LET'S PLAY DOCTOR

Also by Mark Leyner and Billy Goldberg, M.D.

Why Do Men Have Nipples?
Why Do Men Fall Asleep After Sex?

LET'S PLAY DOCTOR

The Instant Guide to Walking,
Talking, and Probing Like a Real M.D.

Mark Leyner and Billy Goldberg, M.D.

THREE RIVERS PRESS • NEW YORK

Library of Congress Cataloging-in-Publication Data
Leyner, Mark.
    Let's play doctor / Mark Leyner and Billy Goldberg.—1st ed.
  1. Medicine—Miscellanea.   I. Goldberg, Billy.   II. Title.
    R706.L478 2008
    610—dc22   2008039916

ISBN 978-0-307-34598-1

Printed in the United States of America

Design by Kay Schuckhart/Blond on Pond

10 9 8 7 6 5 4 3 2 1

First Edition

You can't become a great doctor without a pantheon of great teachers. We dedicate this book to all the scholars who inspired us throughout the years.

Match these inspirational academics with the film or television show in which they were featured:

1. Ms. Norbury
   (Tina Fey)

2. John Kimble
   (Arnold Schwarzenegger)

3. Edna Krabappel
   (as self)

4. The Economics Teacher
   (Ben Stein)

5. John Keating
   (Robin Williams)

6. Mr. Hand
   (Ray Walston)

7. Mr. Holland
   (Richard Dreyfuss)

8. Mark Thackeray
   (Sidney Poitier)

9. Ross Geller
   (David Schwimmer)

10. Prof. Grady Tripp
    (Michael Douglas)

11. Charles W. Kingsfield Jr.
    (John Houseman)

12. Steve
    (Steve)

13. Kermit the Frog
    (as self)

14. Gabe Kotter
    (Gabe Kaplan)

15. Prof. Henry Higgins
    (Rex Harrison)

16. Mr. Feeny
    (William Daniels)

A. *The Nutty Professor*

B. *Blues Clues*

C. *Mr. Holland's Opus*

D. *Boy Meets World*

E. *The White Shadow*

F. *School of Rock*

G. *Grease*

H. *Election*

I. *My Fair Lady*

J. *The Absent-Minded Professor*

K. *Up the Down Staircase*

L. *Mean Girls*

M. *Clueless*

N. *Carrie*

O. *Degrassi Junior High*

P. *Room 222*

17. Dr. Diane Turner
    (Sally Kellerman)

Q. *Good Will Hunting*

18. Sylvia Barrett
    (Sandy Dennis)

R. *Kindergarten Cop*

19. Pete Dixon
    (Lloyd Haynes)

S. *Blackboard Jungle*

20. Ken Reeves
    (Ken Howard)

T. *To Sir, With Love*

21. Jean Brodie
    (Maggie Smith)

U. *Friends*

22. Mr. Wendell Hall
    (Wallace Shawn)

V. *90210*

23. Richard Dadier
    (Glenn Ford)

W. *Welcome Back, Kotter*

24. Annie Sullivan
    (Anne Bancroft)

X. *The Simpsons*

25. Prof. Gerald Lambeau
    (Stellan Skarsgård)

Y. *Harry Potter and the Prisoner of Azkaban*

26. Prof. Ned Brainard
    (Fred MacMurray)

Z. *Back to School*

27. Jim McAllister
    (Matthew Broderick)

AA. *Ferris Bueller's Day Off*

28. Miss Evelyn Togar
    (Mary Woronov)

BB. *Fast Times at Ridgemont High*

29. Dewey Finn
    (Jack Black)

CC. *Sesame Street*

30. Dr. Frank Bryant
    (Michael Caine)

DD. *Wonder Boys*

31. Prof. Julius Kelp
    (Jerry Lewis)

EE. *The Miracle Worker*

32. Miss Collins
    (Betty Buckley)

FF. *Dead Poets Society*

33. Mr. Raditch
    (Dan Woods)

GG. *The Prime of Miss Jean Brodie*

34. Brenda Walsh
    (Shannen Doherty)

HH. *The Paper Chase*

35. Principal McGee
    (Eve Arden)

II. *Rock 'n' Roll High School*

36. Prof. Remus Lupin
    (David Thewlis)

JJ. *Educating Rita*

For answer key, see page 224.

CONTENTS

INTRODUCTION: WELCOME TO THE WHY DO MEN
HAVE NIPPLES SCHOOL OF MEDICINE   1

CHAPTER 1:   BUILDING YOUR MED SCHOOL BRAIN
How to Be More Smarter *Now!*   9

CHAPTER 2:   TALKING THE BODY TALK
Anatomy 101   53

CHAPTER 3:   DIAGNOSE THIS!
Acne or Leprosy—You Make the Call   94

CHAPTER 4:   DO-IT-YOURSELF MEDICINE
Appendectomies-R-Us   112

CHAPTER 5:   MEDICAL MANNERS, ETHICS, AND MORALITY
At Least Pretend to Be Professional   134

CHAPTER 6:   FINAL EXAM
Test Your Dr. "Skills"   177

COMMENCEMENT ADDRESS
Today, You Are a Real Fake Doctor   203

ACKNOWLEDGMENTS   209

LET'S PLAY DOCTOR

When our first book, *Why Do Men Have Nipples?*, hit the best-seller list, we found ourselves atop a peculiar category in the *New York Times*: "Advice, How-To and Miscellaneous." "Miscellaneous" seemed to suit us perfectly—we're two of the most miscellaneous people you could imagine. But "advice"? "How-to"? The idea that we'd ever be in a position to offer insights to people about anything important seemed laughable at best, and downright dangerous at worst.

INTRODUCTION

Welcome to the
Why Do Men Have Nipples
School of Medicine

Yet, thanks to the success of our books, *Why Do Men Have Nipples?* and the follow-up *Why Do Men Fall Asleep After Sex?*, we became two of the nation's leading medical experts. Experts? Leyner isn't even a doctor. Come to think of it, we're not exactly sure how Leyner was qualified to answer medical questions of *any* sort in the first place. But that didn't stop him. And it doesn't have to stop you!

You ever notice these days how everyone seems to want to act and sound like a doctor? *Everyone* seems to love coming off like some sort of medical guru. With Sanjay Gupta, WebMD, and Google, everyone can quote medical information, tell you how to cure your cold, treat your tennis elbow, and sleep-train your newborn. Everyone—not just doctors—has a medical opinion these days. That's because *everyone* likes telling other people what to do, not just us! And, if Leyner can anoint himself a Real Fake Doctor, so can you! *Let's Play Doctor* is your easy-to-follow, fun-to-use, one-stop shop for acting, sounding, and thinking like a real M.D.

Welcome to Bedside Manor: The Why Do Men Have Nipples School of Medicine. This revolutionary volume is a condensed yet comprehensive curriculum that will make actually attending medical school seem like some quaint and obsolete thing of the distant past. Why pay enormous sums in tuition, waste four years of your life, and find yourself hopelessly in debt, when for only $14.95, you get the world's *easiest* and most comprehensive guide to livin' la vida doctor?

FIVE SIMPLE RULES TO SUMMON YOUR INNER INTERN

1. Watch a lot of medical TV!

You'll learn the secret techniques and confidence-building tics and mannerisms of the great television doctors. You'll learn to effect the grave integrity of Dr. Ben Casey, the empathic charm of Dr. Kildare, the warmth and caring of Dr. Marcus Welby, the dogged persistence of Dr. Quincy, the boyish élan and precocious intelligence of Doogie Hauser, the disarming humor of Dr. Cliff Huxtable, the eccentric diagnostic acumen of Dr. Gregory House, and the borderline inappropriate sexuality of Dr. McDreamy.

2. Get some sort of degree.

Anything that allows you to put letters after your name works. Nobody really knows what they mean anyway. At the Why Do Men Have Nipples School of Medicine, you'll have your choice of receiving a B.G. or M.L. (Bachelor of Goldberg or Master of Leyner).

3. Always quote the medical literature.

We suggest easy catchphrases like "Current research shows . . . ," "The evidence indicates . . . ," or "Recent studies demonstrate . . ." Anything that you add after is irrefutable.

4. Use big, polysyllabic, esoteric medical lingo whenever possible.

Anyone call tell a person that he's got an itchy butt, but looking a man straight in the eye and informing him that the etiology of his condition is an acute idiopathic case of pruritus ani gives you immediate doctorlike mojo! Remember, when it comes to laying on the arcane jargon, more is more.

5. Know your patients and pander shamelessly to them.

Remember: Being pandered to is empowering and life-affirming! It's actually true that the more people like you, the less likely it is that they'll sue you. Smiling is a lot easier than being smart.

Now all you have to do is read a few random pages of *Let's Play Doctor* here and there (while you sit on the toilet or wait for your name to be called at the DMV) and you'll be the most informed pseudodoctor at the PTA meeting or in the grocery store. You'll have all the answers when your friends complain about their bright red rashes, impacted earwax, and painful urination. Thanks to this indispensable volume (that will fit easily in your gym bag or the glove compartment of your car), you'll be able to act and sound like a real "doctor," without having to attend medical school, without being awoken in the middle of the night by frantic calls from apocalyptically hypochondriacal patients who've mistaken a zit for some sort of fatal, flesh-eating infection, and without having to spend your day wrist-deep in other people's orifices.

We swear. Cross our hearts and hope to die.

Acting like a doctor doesn't mean driving around in a Porsche Carrera GT with M.D. vanity plates or wearing a big, shiny, sterling-silver stethoscope around your neck like Flavor Flav's clock. It means feeling informed and supremely confident, and being able to simultaneously scare the living shit out of people and gently console them. Isn't it time to find your inner physician? Remember, there's an amateur proctologist in all of us just waiting to come out!

WELCOME, INAUGURAL CLASS!

By turning the page, you officially matriculate in our inaugural class. The ride may be bumpy. So sharpen those pencils, make sure your laptop is fully charged, put your tray tables and seat backs in the upright and locked position. And remember, the contents of your brain may shift in flight.

Class is in session!

CHAPTER 1

S ome of the greatest minds of all time have pondered the power of the brain:

Charles Darwin:

"It is certain that there may be extraordinary mental activity with an extremely small absolute mass of nervous matter: thus the wonderfully diversified instincts, mental powers, and affections of ants are notorious, yet their cerebral ganglia are not so large as the quarter of a small pin's head. Under this point of view, the brain of an ant is one of the most marvelous atoms of matter in the world, perhaps more so than the brain of a man."

(from *The Origin of Species*, 1859)

BUILDING YOUR MED SCHOOL BRAIN

How to Be More Smarter Now!

The Scarecrow from *The Wizard of Oz:*

SCARECROW: I haven't got a brain . . . only straw.

DOROTHY: How can you talk if you haven't got a brain?

SCARECROW: I don't know. . . . But some people without brains do an awful lot of talking . . . don't they? (from the script of the film *The Wizard of Oz*, MGM Studios, 1939)

And of course, Dan Quayle, the forty-fourth vice president of the United States:

"What a terrible thing to have lost one's mind. Or not to have a mind at all."

DO YOU REALLY NEED A "DR. BRAIN"?

If you really went to medical school (instead of just wanting to *act* like you went to medical school), you'd encounter all sorts of incredibly smart, ambitious, and ruthlessly competitive med-school students all vying for perfect scores and the best residencies. To be honest, and Billy can attest to this, this is one of the many ways in which medical school is really annoying. But, if you want to succeed in med school and play at an elite level, you'd better bring your cognitive A-game, baby! And it doesn't end there. Once you're an intern and competing for coveted hospital positions or trying to land jobs with lucrative practices, it's a doc-eat-doc world out there. To succeed at your elaborate acting like a doctor ruse, you have to do the same thing. There are many know-it-alls out there who read a lot and research all sorts of stuff online. That's not enough for the students at Bedside Manor. You need to seem supersharp. You need to display that mental agility, that perspicacity, that number-crunching brain-brawn that will impress your friends and family and intimidate your rivals. We can help.

SO HOW DO I KNOW IF I'M SMART ENOUGH TO ACT LIKE A DOCTOR?

Well . . . uh . . . you bought this book, right? No offense, but that kinda answers the question. Let's be honest. If you were a brilliant, erudite person, you probably would have bought Leo Tolstoy's *Anna Karenina* or Gilles Deleuze and Félix Guattari's *A Thousand Plateaus: Capitalism and Schizophrenia,* not a book called *Let's Play Doctor.* So, chances are you're probably not exceptionally bright. You're probably only average,

OK? Don't sweat it. You're better off being average. Exceptionally smart people tend to be unhappy and crazy and suicidal. Who would you rather be: Vincent van Gogh or Ryan Seacrest? Sylvia Plath or Rachael Ray? No-brainer, right? The key to getting smarter, or at the very least, just not getting any dumber as time goes on, is to be prepared to work. Is it possible to actually change your brain? you ask. Does flexing those mental muscles really work? And does that venerable gym maxim "Use it or lose it" apply to the ol' noodle? The answer is . . . *duh* . . . Yes! It's all you, baby!

Neuroscientists today believe that learning and memory rely upon changes at neuron-to-neuron synapses called long-term potentiation (LTP). LTP involves patterns of synaptic strengthening and weakening, and facilitates the communication between connected neurons, thus forming memories.

A recent study by Brown University neuroscientists (see, we're quoting a study—don't we sound very doctorlike?) demonstrated that learning uses LTP to produce changes in the synaptic connections between brain cells that are vital to the acquisition and storage of new information. When the researchers taught rats a new motor skill, they discovered that the animals' brains had actually changed—the strength of the synapses between neurons in the motor cortex of their brains had increased! Pump it, Willard!

Plus, a new study conducted by researchers at Rush University Medical Center in Chicago (here we go again) shows that people who engaged in cognitively stimulating activities were less likely to suffer from dementia later in life. Major studies conducted by the National Institute of Mental Health in Philadelphia, Duke University, and the National Institute on Aging all demonstrate that mental decline with aging is *not* inevitable.

The human brain is able to continually adapt and "rewire" itself. And there's an ever-increasing body of scientific opinion that you can take steps in your life to actually improve your *brain power,* and that lack of mental exercise and stimulation can result in mental decline.

So, OK . . . Do you want a gym-honed brain? A brain that'll look good nude? A six-pack cerebral cortex?

Here we recommend some lifestyle changes, exercises, and new hobbies.

Warning: These are *not* the typically lame puzzles and "brainteasers" you'll find in other self-help books. Those are for pussies. These are only for people who are serious about working hard and having SUPER-HOT DOCTOR brains. Also, the answers appear pretty close to the questions on the following pages. That doesn't mean, however, that you can cheat.

WARM-UP EXERCISES

1. Beginner

Some months have 30 days, some have 31. How many months have 28 days?

Answer: They all do! (LOL!!!!)

2. Intermediate

Three people—Billy Bob, Henry Ng, and Little J.—check into a motel in Manchester, England. They pay £30 to the manager and go to their room to smoke crack. The manager suddenly remembers that the room rate is £25 and gives £5 to the bellboy to return to the people. On the way to the room the bellboy reasons that £5 would be difficult to share among three people, so he pockets £2 and gives £1 to each person. Now each person paid £10 and got back £1. So they paid £9 each, totaling £27. The bellboy has £2, totaling £29. Where is the missing £1?

Answer: The trick here is to be very careful about what you add together. Originally, the three degenerate drifters paid £30, they each received back £1, and thus they now have only paid £27. Of this £27, £25 went to the manager for the room and £2 went to the bellboy.

3. **Advanced**

The speed of sound is 343 meters/second (at sea level, or 770 mph). Without using a calculator, multiply this number by the factor of Jessica Simpson's bra size, and then divide by the number of concussions suffered by Troy Aikman during his career with the Dallas Cowboys.

Answer: 343 × 34D ÷ 10 concussions = 1166.2

4. **Neurosurgeon**

One night, two fabulously rich Mexican telenovela stars, Victor Perez Garcia Alejandro Ignacio Figueroa and Manuel Hernandez Badillo Garcia Arellano Bravo, are watching *The World's Strongest Man on TV*. Mariusz Pudzianowski has just won the Keg Toss—throwing ten 50-pound kegs over a 14-foot-16-inch-high steel wall in a time of 42.80 seconds. In his exuberance, one of the two friends inadvertently bounces on the remote, changing the channel to a Classic TV rerun showing Eva Gabor playing Twister with Johnny Carson on the *Tonight Show* on May 3, 1966. Victor Perez Garcia Alejandro

Ignacio Figueroa has an epiphany: "Let's go play Twister at the Four Corners Monument which marks the quadripoint where the states of Arizona, Colorado, New Mexico, and Utah meet." "I love the way your mind works!" exults Manuel Hernandez Badillo Garcia Arellano Bravo. "Let's open up the safe—we'll need lots of money for the trip!" Manuel fumbles desperately with the lock for several minutes. "Shit!" he says. "I forgot the combination."

Help these two handsome amigos remember the combination, so they can get their money and go play Twister together at the Four Corners Monument! Here's a hint. The combination is the length (in centimeters) of Ron Jeremy's penis; the total calories in two Skittles; and the number of times the word "fuck" is uttered in the film *Scarface*, minus 3 times the distance of the longest field goal in NFL history, plus the number of times the letter *n* appears in the names of the Jonas Brothers.

Answer: Ron Jeremy's penis is 25 centimeters. A single Skittle contains 4.5 calories. So two Skittles contain a total of 9 calories. According to IMDb, the word "fuck" is used 226 times in *Scarface*. Jason Elam of the Denver Broncos and Tom Dempsey of the New Orleans Saints share the NFL record for longest field goal, which is 63 yards. The letter n appears 5 times in the names of Joe Jonas, Nick Jonas, and Kevin Jonas. Multiply 3 times 63 for a product of 189. Subtract 189 from 226 for a remainder of 37, and add 5 for a sum of 42.

You got it! The lock's combination is: 25-9-42.

5. **Lightning Round**

    Give yourself 15 seconds to answer each of the following tricky brain-puzzlers:

    • Why is there so much suffering in life?

    • Can the world's wealth ever be equitably distributed?

    • Is there a logical nexus between particle physics and cosmology?

    • Given the fundamental physical laws of the universe, would not an extraterrestrial civilization develop precisely the same mathematics as ours? If not, what possible basis could there be for differences?

    • What do chickens think we taste like?

OK, now that you're all warmed up, you're all set. Read on . . . and embrace your DOCTOR BRAIN. What follows is a series of tips, tricks, Q & A, and additional exercises that will enhance your gray muscle.

NUMBERS ON THE BRAIN

• **100,000,000,000:** estimated number of brain cells in the average adult brain

• **10 billion:** estimated number of brain cells lost by the average adult over a lifetime

• **200 million:** estimated number of additional brain cells lost by an average Alzheimer's patient

• **85,000:** estimated number of brain cells lost by the average adult each day

• **200 million:** miles of neurons formed if every brain cell in the average adult brain were arranged end to end

• **50:** estimated number of brain cells regenerated by the average adult each day

THE ENHANCE YOUR BRAIN DIET

Sure you could load up on all the grub that supposedly boosts brain functioning, like ginkgo biloba, omega-3s, choline (the fatlike B vitamin found in eggs), antioxidant-rich foods like blueberries, red grapes, and green tea. But we say, why not just eat what the geniuses ate? It worked for them!

Here are the favorite foods of some of history's most brilliant minds. Chow down and watch your IQ skyrocket!

- Wolfgang Amadeus Mozart: black coffee, veal cutlets, *leberknödel* (liver dumplings)

- Ludwig van Beethoven: *eintopf* (a traditional German stew), and macaroni and cheese

- Albert Einstein: spaghetti and fettuccini

- Stephen Hawking: Indian food, especially chicken jalfrezi

- Friedrich Nietzsche (perhaps the greatest of history's Four Great Freds: Nietzsche, MacMurray, Mertz, and Flintstone)—the man who wrote "That which does not kill us makes us stronger" (no, Kanye West did not write that) . . . yes, the most brilliant philosophical aphorist of all time ("I only believe in a God who knows how to dance" and "In Heaven, all the interesting people are missing")—for a time subsisted almost entirely on warm milk, but he came to cherish, above all else, an expertly prepared osso buco alla Milanese (braised veal shank)

- Michael Faraday—the nineteenth-century English chemist who discovered electromagnetic induction—loved nothing better than a Taco Bell Chalupa Supreme (chicken), which he'd wash down with a flagon of Sunny D (OK, this isn't exactly true, but the rest were)

MEDICAL SCHOOL FLASHBACK
The Stethoscope

She is a middle-aged Asian woman and my first clinical experience. I follow Dr. B into the exam room where the woman sits slumped in a chair. She smiles easily as we enter and tells us that she has the flu. Mrs. S suffers from Graves' disease, which is an autoimmune disease in which the body creates antibodies that mimic thyroid-stimulating hormone. As a result, the thyroid is constantly activated, or overactive. Dr. B asks how she is doing and what she would like to talk about. Mrs. S explains that she was advised to see her doctor by the endocrinologist who has been giving her radio-iodine treatment to "kill" her thyroid. Her energy is low and she tells us she's been tired for a few weeks. I later learn it is an effect of the treatment because the thyroid activity is diminishing.

Dr. B tells me to listen to her heart and report back to him as he steps out of the room. Having never actually used my stethoscope before, I place it in my ears and apply the metal piece to her chest. Meanwhile, I cannot hear a thing. I move the piece around on her chest, hunting for any sign of a heartbeat. The only noise I detect is a soft beating sound that I quickly discern is my own heart due to the synchronized thumping I also feel in my ears. My excitement quickly vanishes. I readjust the placement of the piece on her chest . . . . nothing. At this point I'm discouraged and praying that Dr. B will be gentle on me, as it's apparent I have absolutely no idea what I'm doing.

He returns to the exam room and I announce with a grimace on my face, "I think my stethoscope is broken." He smiles really wide and takes it from me, places it in his ears, and tells me to press harder. Meanwhile, I observe the direction he placed it in his ears and stymie a laugh as I realize I had the thing in backward.

—Dr. Langley Partridge, emergency medicine resident

Is it true that breakfast can make people smarter?

Breakfast is key. It can be your Brain's Banquet. Your brain runs on a steady intake of glucose, and skipping breakfast has been shown to reduce students' performances at school and people's ability to function effectively at the job.

Your brain is a part of your body—a very special part no doubt, but a body part nonetheless. And like the rest of your body, it needs good food, not just junk calories. Recent research showed clearly that children who gorged on a breakfast of soda and sugary snack foods performed at the level of an average 70-year-old in tests of memory and attention.

Eggs are a particularly *smart* choice. Eggs are rich in choline, which your body uses to produce the neurotransmitter acetylcholine. (One whole large egg provides 112 mg of choline.) Low levels of acetylcholine have been associated with Alzheimer's disease, and studies have suggested that increasing your dietary intake of choline may slow age-related memory loss.

Here are some other choline-rich foods:

- **Beef liver:** pan-fried, 100 grams (about 3.5 ounces) = 418 milligrams

- **Beef, ground, 80% lean/20% fat:** 3.5-ounce patty = 81 milligrams

- **Cauliflower:** 3/4 cup cooked = 62 milligrams

- **Navy beans:** 1/2 cup cooked = 48 milligrams

- **Tofu:** 100 grams (about 3.5 ounces) = 28 milligrams

- **Almonds, sliced:** 1/2 cup = 26 milligrams

- **Peanut butter:** 2 tablespoons = 20 milligrams

Can blueberries really make you smart?
Eating blueberries and running on a wheel two hours a day just might turn you into Einstein . . . or at least a very, very smart version of Stuart Little.

Epicatechin, a natural compound found in blue-berries (as well as in tea, grapes, and cocoa), enhances memory in mice, according to recent research published in the *Journal of Neuroscience*. This effect increased further when the mice also exercised regularly. Mice fed a typical diet were compared with those fed a diet supplemented with epicatechin. Half the mice in each group were allowed to run on a wheel for two hours each day. After a month, the mice were trained to find a platform hidden in a pool of water. Those that both exercised and ate the epicatechin diet remembered the location of the platform longer than the other mice.

Scientists studying their brains found that these mice had greater blood vessel growth in the dentate gyrus and had developed more mature nerve cells, suggesting an enhanced ability of the cells to communicate.

What's so magical about antioxidants?

Antioxidants, including beta-carotene and vitamins C and E, are thought to help keep the brain on its A-game by getting rid of damaging free radicals. Scientists from the University of California at Irvine found that a diet high in antioxidants improved the cognitive skills of aging beagles. You don't want to be outsmarted by a bunch of aging beagles, do you?! Blueberries and strawberries are paricularly good—and good-tasting—sources of antioxidants. A new study conducted by the

United States Department of Agriculture, the Human Nutrition Research Center on Aging, and Tufts University shows that rats given a diet supplemented with blueberries and strawberries showed reversals of age-related declines in neuronal signal transduction, and cognitive and motor behavioral deficits.

Can yogurt help my . . . (oh, I forgot what I was going to ask).

Some yummy blueberry yogurt might be just the thing for your hungry brain. Studies conducted by the U.S. military have shown that tyrosine—an amino acid abundant in yogurt—becomes depleted when you're stressed out and that supplementing your intake can improve alertness and memory. That may be because tyrosine is necessary for the production of the neurotransmitters dopamine and noradrenaline.

What about fish oil?

Let's not forget those omega-3 fatty acids—particularly docosahexaenoic acid (DHA). There's mounting evidence that DHA also seems to help prevent or at least delay age-related dementia. Recent studies reveal that older mice from a strain genetically altered to develop Alzheimer's had 70 percent less of the amyloid plaques associated with the disease when fed a high-DHA diet.

Are there any foods that make people dumber?

Foods? Like a steady diet of Peeps, pork rinds, and Kool-Aid? This might not be so great for your mental health, or your physical health either, for that matter. But specific foods that might cause brain damage? Except for foods tainted with toxins or poisons, probably not.

A study conducted by Ann-Charlotte E. Granholm of the Medical University of South Carolina in Charleston showed that trans fats adversely affected rats' learning ability. The brains of the animals showed signs of damage in the hippocampus—the brain's memory center. These are very preliminary studies, and, of course, it's not clear at all if a similar effect can be demonstrated in human beings. That being said, trans fats introduce a host of other health issues, which have all been well documented in the press. Stay away from packaged baked goods. . . .

If Mama didn't nurse me, am I doomed to be dumb?

Feeling especially dim-witted lately? Maybe you didn't get enough of Mama's milk. According to the results of a study published in the *Archives of General Psychiatry*, prolonged breast-feeding results in improved scores on intelligence tests in childhood. Researchers in Belarus found that breast-fed 6½-year-olds scored significantly higher on tests of vocabulary, word matching, and verbal IQ. Was it the lactation or the love? In other words, the question might arise as to whether the differences were caused by chemical constituents of breast milk or the physical and social interactions between mother and child. But lead author Dr. Michael S. Kramer is unequivocal: "It's the breast-feeding that's doing it," he avers.

If you're feeling a little hazy in the head, don't try to hustle an extra squirt from your nursing wife. There's no evidence that breast milk has any effect on intelligence when consumed by an adult.

SPANKING THE MENTAL MONKEY

Now that you know what to eat to create a DOCTOR brain, here are additional tricks. This is a highly effective form of mental multitasking that will really work *both* sides of your brain!

Each hemisphere of the brain is more active during certain activities and behaviors. The left brain may be more dominant for calculations, math, and logical abilities. Evidence suggests that we tend to have orgasms with the right side of our brain.

Start by reading a college algebra or trigonometry book *while* masturbating. Imagine the excellent workout your brain will get if, as you're writhing with pleasure, you're simultaneously trying to solve this: The pressure P of enclosed gas varies directly as the absolute temperature T and inversely as the volume V. If 500 ft^3 of gas yields a pressure of 10 lb/ft^2 at a temperature of 300 K (absolute temperature), what will be the pressure of the same gas if the volume is decreased to 300 ft^3 and the temperature increased to 360 K?

Or do a couple of sets of these hemisphere-isolating exercises:

LEFT-BRAIN ACTIVITIES	RIGHT-BRAIN ACTIVITIES
1. Figure out how big a tip to leave a cute but incompetent waitress.	1. Forget the big tip; scrawl her a love poem on your napkin.
2. Give three-hour lecture on the laws of thermodynamics.	2. Give a twenty-minute rambling soliloquy on what's a sappier song: "I Just Called to Say I Love You" by Stevie Wonder or Boyz II Men's "It's So Hard to Say Goodbye to Yesterday."
3. Play Scrabble with your in-laws.	3. Play doctor with your best friend's sister.

MORE FAVORITE FOODS OF GENIUSES

Thomas Jefferson: ice cream, pancakes, spoon bread

Walt Whitman: buckwheat cakes, beef steak, oysters

Thomas Alva Edison: apple dumplings

LaToya Jackson: hot tamales and strawberry twizzlers

TRAIN THAT BRAIN—MULTITASK FOR MAXIMUM BRAIN POWER

You know how difficult it can be to pay attention to something you're reading while someone else is talking to you? It's a form of mental multitasking that involves cognitive dissonance—holding conflicting thoughts in the mind at the same time. It's actually great resistance training for the mind.

Here are a couple of excellent exercises that utilize cognitive dissonance:

Sit on the couch with a nice cup of green tea and the latest issue of *Miniature Donkey Talk Magazine* (or the more medically focused *Journal of Veterinary Diagnostic Investigation*). Relax. Start reading the article entitled

"Facts Regarding Biotin and Other Hoof Supplements." Have your workout buddy enter the room and start explaining the plot of the movie *Saw* to you ("OK . . . there's this, like, industrial washroom and there's this photographer and this doctor and they're chained by their ankles to pipes and there's this corpse holding a revolver and from this microcassette, the doctor learns that he has to kill the photographer or his wife and his daughter will be killed, and there's this psycho guy named Zep Hindle and he used to be an orderly in the hospital where the doctor worked," etc.).

The key here is to pay careful attention to both your article on donkey-hoof supplements *and* the convoluted plot summary of *Saw*.

(By the way, for any of you who are interested in donkeys of any size, *Miniature Donkey Talk Magazine* is the premiere donkey magazine in the country. Julian Cable, DVM, has called it "The best donkey magazine being published!" Here is their website: http://www.qis.net/minidonk/mdt.htm.)

Now add even more dissonance—maybe your wife arrives and starts droning on interminably about some summer rental for $15,000 for two weeks in Bayhead, New Jersey.

Split that focus three ways! Pay attention to everything:

the hoof supplements, the Jigsaw Killer, and the beach house.

Do 3 sets of 10 reps.

You got it, Dude. . . . It's all you!

If you want to be an ER doctor like Dr. Billy, you gotta be able to multitask.

Here are some real facts about emergency physicians being interrupted:

- They are interrupted 30.7 times in every 180-minute cycle.

- They are interrupted 9.7 times per hour, while office-based physicians are interrupted 3.9 times per hour.

- Emergency physicians spend two-thirds of their time managing multiple patients (three or more).

READING COMPREHENSION

Reading—for speed and comprehension—is one of the best ways to give your mind a heavy-duty workout. As a student at Bedside Manor: The Why Do Men Have Nipples School of Medicine, your reading load is far less than that of the average med student. Basically, all you have to read is this book! However, you need to read it for maximum understanding, so you'll be able to embrace your inner doctor faster, but also be able to tell all your friends how great the book is so they'll buy it too.

Try reading the following passage as rapidly as you possibly can and then answering the multiple-choice questions to the best of your ability. You'll feel that brain-burn!

Once upon a time, there were a brother and a sister, and they loved each other dearly—not in any perverse, incestuous way; they just really got along and shared many interests. (For example, they were both huge fans of Michael Flatley and Irish step-dancing, and had both seen Riverdance *more than 30 times!) Their mother, a pole-dancing attorney from Long Island, had vanished years ago. Their cruel stepmother wouldn't feed them, so they were forced to forage in the dark forest or else they would surely starve to death.*

One day, after wandering futilely through the woods, and not finding a thing to eat, they came upon a squalid little shack. Their poor empty stomachs were making all sorts of plaintive sounds. It is hard to overemphasize how squalid and disgusting this shack was. It looked more like an outdoor latrine or a Porta-John than a place where someone could actually live. But they were desperate, so they knocked on the door. When an enchanted prince opened the door, the brother and sister couldn't believe their eyes.

Somehow, what had appeared from the outside to be this abject aluminum outhouse was magically on the inside a spacious and elegant pied-à-terre. The kitchen was especially gorgeous, with a terrazzo floor, a marble and brushed-nickel island, Miele and Sub-Zero appliances, etc. Something was cooking that smelled so good that it made the brother's and sister's mouths water. The enchanted prince took a huge roasting pan out from the oven and there lying on a bed of fennel-flavored risotto and caramelized onions was the evil stepmother.

"Please don't cook our stepmother!" the two children cried out.

"But you two are so hungry, and she has been so cruel to you both," replied the prince.

"We know, but it's not her fault that she's a sad and bitter person."

The enchanted prince was so moved by the magnanimity of the hungry little children that he turned the roasting stepmother into a loving and voluptuous Asian woman.

And the four of them lived in that strange pied-à-terre forever, happy and content.

1.   How does the author intend you to feel?

  A. Angry about cattle flatulence and teenage obesity

  B. Morally invigorated about the intrinsic goodness of most people

C. Horny and wistfully nostalgic about your own adolescence

D. Confused, itchy, and nauseous

2. **Which words do *not* appear in this passage?**
   A. Pied-à-terre

   B. Plaintive

   C. Caramelized onions

   D. Anal bleaching

3. **What happened to the brother and sister's father?**
   A. He's a loser—who gives a fuck? He obviously doesn't care enough about his own children to even look for them now that they've been missing, according to the passage, "forever." Plus, he doesn't have the balls to confront the enchanted prince who intended to cook and cannibalize his wife and then instead turned her into his sex-crazed concubine.

4. **Meredith Baxter has appeared in:**
   A. *My Breast*

   B. *Ben*

C. *I Married a Miniature Donkey: The Janet Mastrobono Story*

D. *A Woman Scorned: The Betty Broderick Story*

Answer Key

1. D

2. D

3. A

4. A, B, and D

NEXUS—THE GAME

Here's a great game guaranteed to enhance your mental acuity. We call it Nexus. It requires you to form a series of links that connect two seemingly disparate and unrelated names. You'll need your workout partner for this one. Here are two examples that will demonstrate how to play.

I present two names to my workout partner: *Charles Bronson* and *Haile Selassie*. My workout partner will then figure out how to establish the necessary links that will logically connect these two figures.

OK, let's see . . . Charles Bronson starred as crime-fighting vigilante Paul Kersey in the 1974 film *Death Wish*. . . . The sound track to *Death Wish* was composed by jazz pianist Herbie Hancock. . . . In 2005, Herbie Hancock released an album of duets called *Possibilities,* which included a song with Christina Aguilera called "A Song for You" (which was nominated for a Grammy Award). . . . Christina Aguilera did the voice for a Rastafarian jellyfish in the animated film *Shark Tale* . . . and Rastafarians consider whom to be the religious symbol of God incarnate? . . . The former emperor of Ethiopia, Haile Selassie!

Do a leaping chest-bump as you yell "Nexus!"

Now it's your partner's turn to provide the names. He says, "Billy Idol and George Jefferson."

Damn, bro . . . that's a tough one!

Hmmmm . . . I got it. Billy Idol played himself in the 1998 romantic comedy *The Wedding Singer,* starring Adam Sandler. . . . Adam Sandler played Theo Huxtable's friend Smitty on *The Cosby Show.* . . . On *The Cosby Show,* the character of Denise Huxtable was played by Lisa Bonet. . . . On her twentieth birthday, Lisa Bonet eloped with singer Lenny Kravitz. . . . Lenny Kravitz is the son of Roxie Roker, the actress who played Helen Willis in the 1970s sitcom *The Jeffersons* . . . which, of course, starred the inimitable Sherman Hemsley as George Jefferson!

Leaping chest-bump! NEXUS!!!

Neurogenesis (the process by which new nerve cells are generated) has never been this much fun!!! OK, ready to try a couple yourself? Here we go, let's get MEDICAL!

Alexander Fleming, the legendary Scottish biologist who, in 1928, discovered the antibiotic penicillin from the fungus *Penicillium notatum,* and actress/sex symbol **Pamela Anderson.**

Solution: Alexander Fleming was awarded the Nobel Prize in Physiology or Medicine in 1945. After his sudden death in 1955 from a heart attack, his widow, Dr. Amalia Koutsouri-Vourekas, presented his Nobel Prize medal to the Savage Club—a London gentlemen's club, where Fleming was a member. A prominent member of the Savage Club was the British actor Sir Peter Ustinov. In 1951, Ustinov starred in a movie called *Quo Vadis,* in which he played the Roman emperor Nero. Nero's maternal uncle was the tyrannical, sexually perverse, and epileptic Caligula. In the 1979 movie *Caligula* (financed by Bob Guccione), the eponymous emperor was played by actor Malcolm McDowell. McDowell was married to actress Mary Steenburgen (they divorced in 1990). Steenburgen is currently married to Ted Danson, who played Sam Malone on the hit series *Cheers.* The Cheers theme song, "Where Everybody Knows Your Name," was written and performed by Gary Portnoy and Judy Hart Angelo, who also wrote the theme song for the series *Punky Brewster,* whose title character was portrayed by Soleil Moon Frye.

From 2000 to 2003, Frye played Roxie King in *Sabrina the Teenage Witch*, starring Melissa Joan Hart as Sabrina Spellman. In 2007, Hart starred in an enormously successful ABC Family Original Movie called *Holiday in Handcuffs*, in the lead role of Trudie Chandler. Also appearing in *Holiday in Handcuffs* was an actress by the name of Vanessa Lee Evigan, who, from 2001 to 2007, dated Linkin Park drummer Rob Bourdon. Linkin Park's front man Chester Bennington was the guest vocalist on Mötley Crüe's 2005 remake of "Home Sweet Home." Mötley Crüe's drummer is the notorious Tommy Lee, whose girlfriend is, of course, the iconically voluptuous **Pamela Anderson**.

Marie Curie, the legendary scientist who discovered radium and developed its therapeutic properties—the only woman to have won two Nobel Prizes, and the only person to have won Nobel Prizes in two different scientific fields (physics and chemistry)—and three-time Academy Award nominee, three-time Golden Globe Award winner, and fervent Scientology adherent **Tom Cruise.**

Solution: Marie Curie isolated radium from the mineral pitchblende. One of the world's most significant sources of pitchblende is Great Bear Lake in the Northwest Territories of Canada. The only community on Great Bear Lake is Deline. Deline is primarily populated by the indigenous Sahtu Dene people (who speak a language called North Slavey). The most renowned Dene entertainer in the world is a singer/songwriter by the name of Leela Gilday, who, in 2007, won the Juno Award for Aboriginal Recording of the Year for her second album, *Sedzé*. In 2004, the Juno Award for Aboriginal Recording was awarded to Susan Aglukark for her album *Big Feeling*. Two of Aglukark's songs ("Never Be the Same" and "One Turn Deserves Another") were featured on the television series *Dawson's Creek*, which aired on the WB Television Network from 1998 to 2003. *Dawson's Creek* starred the actress Katie Holmes, who played the character Josephine "Joey" Lynn Potter. Katie Holmes is, of course, married to three-time Academy Award nominee, three-time Golden Globe Award winner, and fervent Scientology adherent **Tom Cruise.**

Now, for EXTRA CREDIT, try **Marie Curie** and . . . actress/sex symbol **Pamela Anderson**!

Marie Curie isolated radium from the mineral pitchblende. One of the world's most significant sources of pitchblende is Great Bear Lake in the Northwest Territories of Canada. The only community on Great Bear Lake is Deline. Deline is primarily populated by the indigenous Sahtu Dene people (who speak a language called North Slavey). The most renowned Dene entertainer in the world is a singer/songwriter by the name of Leela Gilday, who, in 2007, won the Juno Award for Aboriginal Recording of the Year for her second album, *Sedzé*. In 2004, the Juno Award for Aboriginal Recording was awarded to Susan Aglukark for her album *Big Feeling*. Two of Aglukark's songs ("Never Be the Same" and "One Turn Deserves Another") were featured on the television series *Dawson's Creek,* which aired on the WB Television Network from 1998 to 2003. *Dawson's Creek* starred the actress Mary-Margaret Humes, who played the title character's mother, Gail Leery. In 1981, Humes had a role in Mel Brooks's *History of the World, Part I,* portraying the Vestal Virgin, Miriam. Making a cameo appearance in *History of the World, Part I* as himself was *Playboy* magazine publisher Hugh Hefner. On Saturday, April 5, 2008, Hefner, at his eighty-second birthday party at the Palms Fantasy Towers in Las Vegas, Nevada, was given a naked lap dance by none other than the iconically voluptuous actress/sex symbol **Pamela Anderson.**

Nexus Suggestions for Home Study

• Dr. Jack Kevorkian and Samantha Ronson

• Maimonides and Miley Cyrus

- Dr. Sigmund Freud and Kelly Osbourne

- Dr. Jonas Salk and Richie Sambora

Does aerobic exercise make you smarter?

Could Richard Simmons turn out to be not only the overarching genius so many of us have always thought him to be but the great *genius-maker* too?!

It turns out that aerobic exercise is great for your brain! Researchers at the University of Illinois at Urbana-Champaign studied a group of sedentary adults between the ages of 60 and 75, assigning half of them to an aerobic exercise program and the other half to a program of just anaerobic stretching and toning. The scientists found definite improvement in cognitive function in the group that participated in aerobic exercise.

University of Illinois psychology professor Arthur F. Kramer states that "Six months of exercise will buy you a fifteen to twenty percent improvement in memory, decision-making ability, and attention."

Apparently, aerobic activity improves cognitive function by increasing blood flow to the brain and stimulating the production of hormones involved in neurogenesis.

So, all you four-eyed couch potatoes, put down those books. You wanna be brilliant? Put on those candy-striped shorts and crystal-encrusted tank tops and start hopping around like a lunatic!

Are there really drugs that can make you smarter?
Is it just us, or does it seem like, these days, everyone is either struggling to simply keep up or searching for that little something to get a competitive edge?

We are 24-7-365. The two of us are no exception. We are both guilty of swilling espresso as we burn the candle at both ends to finish our new book. But what about these drugs that can instantly improve your cognitive functioning? There's nothing earth-shatteringly radical about the idea of "cognitive enhancers." Whether you're a truck driver, a longshoreman, a French intellectual, a Cosa Nostra capo holding court at his Little Italy social club, a harried reporter at a big-city newspaper, or any one of the roguish characters in Jim Jarmusch's *Coffee and Cigarettes,* everyone knows that a good cup of java and a Marlboro gets the ol' synapses whirring away up there. Caffeine and nicotine are the two old-school cognitive enhancers. Many studies have proven that both help maintain attention, heighten alertness, and, of course, keep people awake. And research has also shown that caffeine possesses cholinergic properties that can enhance higher cognitive functions like short- and long-term memory and perceptual sensitivity.

Two of the drugs used as cognitive enhancers, Donepezil and Tacrine, are acetylcholinesterase inhibitors and were originally approved in the United States for treatment of Alzheimer's disease. (A study published in the journal *Neurology* found that commercial pilots who took 5 milligrams of Donepezil for one month performed better than pilots on a placebo when asked to fly a Cessna 172 on a flight simulator. There was a significant difference between the groups in the effectiveness with which they dealt with emergencies.)

Ritalin is the drug of choice on college campuses for sleep-deprived students struggling to pull all-nighters, complete term papers, and boost concentration during exams. Drugs including Ritalin and Adderall are commonly prescribed to treat attention deficit hyperactivity disorder (ADHD). At recommended doses, these medications can accelerate the central nervous system, heightening concentration and alertness. But as a "smart drug," Ritalin may not be quite so smart. Never mind the fact that sharing prescription medicine is a felony drug offense in most states, but taking excessively high doses of Ritalin can result in adverse reactions and dangerously increase the risk for neurological and heart-related symptoms.

The current superstar among cognitive enhancers is Modafinil—more commonly known as Provigil. The initial indication for Provigil was for use in the treatment of narcolepsy. A secondary FDA indication was to treat something called Shift Work Sleep Disorder (SWSD)—a sleep disorder that affects people who frequently rotate shifts or work nights, schedules that resist the body's natural circadian rhythm. We both know doctors who regularly use Provigil—emergency room physicians are essentially shift workers.

Provigil can keep a person awake and alert for 90 hours straight, with none of the jitteriness, impaired concentration, "rebound effect," or risk of addiction associated with amphetamines or even coffee.

Barbara Sahakian, professor of neuropsychology at the University of Cambridge, who has conducted extensive research on Provigil, has found that it results in greater concentration, faster learning, and increased mental agility. "It may be the first real smart drug," she says. "A lot of people will probably take [it]. I suspect they do already."

Provigil seems to safely bolster alertness for days at a time with few side effects, but its long-term effects have not been sufficiently studied to completely rule out all potential problems. (The French Foreign Legion reportedly used the drug, first developed in France more than a decade ago, during the first Gulf War. We don't know if the drug sped up the legion's legendarily slow 88-step-per-minute marching speed.)

It would be unconscionable (and unconscious) to write about cognitive enhancers without at least mentioning Neurol 1—the "brain-tissue nourishing" drink mix created by Bill Romanowski, who is not a neurologist. Commonly known as "Romo," he is the former NFL linebacker and admitted steroid abuser (he also tried live cell therapy—getting injected with cells from a Scottish black sheep) famous for his viciously unhinged style of play (he crushed the eye socket of tight end Marcus Williams—and Williams was his teammate at the time), and for having suffered up to 20 severe concussions during the course of his career. Neuro 1 is a powder that (according to its creator)—when mixed with water and taken daily—"sharpens memory and recall, improves sports performance, enables you to stay focused and on task longer, supports workout stamina and enhances mood and well-being."

"[It's] for working people who want an edge on the competition," says Romanowski. "You don't need to put on a football helmet and run into people for sixteen years to need this."

Romo plays a gay cowboy in the upcoming movie *Weiners* and an air traffic controller in *Get Smart*.

Sorry for the digression, but it seemed important.

Do any of the newly popular herbal "smart drugs" really work?

The top-selling and most well known herbal "smart drug" on the market is ginkgo biloba. And there is actually a growing body of research confirming that the herb can benefit people with early-stage Alzheimer's disease and multiinfarct dementia. Recent research suggests that it may be, in fact, as effective for such patients as acetylcholinesterase-inhibitor drugs like Donepezil.

What about enhancing cognitive function and memory in healthy people? Here the facts are hazier and current research more contradictory. The Mayo Clinic maintains that further well-designed research is needed before a recommendation can be made.

Great care and consultation with your physician is recommended when you're contemplating the use of any herbal supplement. Although ginkgo biloba is generally well tolerated, there have been multiple reports of bleeding (ranging from simple nosebleeds to life-threatening bleeding in some cases), so it should be used very cautiously in patients on anticoagulant therapy, with known coagulopathy or bleeding disorders, or prior to some surgical or dental procedures.

Are there drugs that can make you dumber?

Many drugs have psychoactive effects—that is, they act upon the central nervous system and alter brain function. These include anesthesia, painkillers, psychiatric drugs, and, of course, recreational drugs.

Questions have arisen lately over whether cholesterol-lowering statin drugs, like Lipitor, have deleterious cognitive side effects, such as befuddled thinking and forgetfulness—i.e., making people stupid. Although hundreds of studies have failed to show a causal link between statins and memory loss, anecdotal reports persist in linking the drugs to memory impairment.

Smoking marijuana often causes temporary problems with memory and learning because the active ingredient in the drug, tetrahydrocannabinoid (THC), disrupts the way nerves fire in the hippocampus.

But of all the various substances we ingest in this society, alcohol has surely wrought the greatest damage to the brains of the most people.

Long-term excessive drinking causes serious neurological damage and memory loss. Some of this damage can repair itself, but some can become permanent. Heavy alcohol use over time actually causes shrinkage in the cortex of the frontal lobe, the locus of higher intellectual functions. In men, this shrinkage generally increases with age. The rate of frontal cortex shrinkage correlates closely with the amount of alcohol consumed. This shrinkage has also been observed in deeper brain regions, including brain structures associated with memory, as well as in the cerebellum, which helps regulate coordination and balance.

The key to avoiding the brain damage associated with alcohol consumption is simple: moderation.

POP QUIZ

Now that you're pumped up and your synapses are exploding like it's the Fourth of July, try solving the following Jimmy Neutron-level problem. (Remember, the ability to think quickly on your feet and effortlessly access esoteric and ultimately useless information is essential to convincing people that you're a real doctor!)

Add the amount of time that Mötley Crüe bassist Nikki Sixx was declared dead after his 1987 heroin overdose to the number of whiskies that poet Dylan Thomas drank at the White Horse Tavern in 1953, and multiply by the age difference between Demi Moore and Ashton Kutcher. Add to that product the *total combined weight* of Jennifer Lopez's and Angelina Jolie's newborn twins and Tila Tequila, then divide by the number of Greek shipping heirs that Paris Hilton has dated. Multiply this quotient by the fraction in which the amount of money British actor Hugh Grant paid Sunset Boulevard prostitute Divine Brown for a blow job is the numerator and the amount of money former New York State governor Eliot Spitzer paid Emperor's Club VIP hooker Ashley Alexandra

Dupré for an hour of sex is the denominator. Add the number of calories in a Hardee's Monster Thickburger and divide by the square root of the number of pairs of pants that Marlon Brando split during the filming of *Mutiny on the Bounty*.

Solution: On December 23, 1987, Mötley Crüe bassist Nikki Sixx was declared dead for **2** minutes after a heroin overdose. Dylan Thomas claimed to have had **18** straight whiskies at the White Horse Tavern in New York City on November 3, 1953. 2 + 18 = **20.** The age difference between Demi Moore and Ashton Kutcher is **15** years. 20 × 15 = **300.** Jennifer Lopez gave birth on February 22, 2008, to fraternal twins, a girl and a boy, Emme Marbiel Muñiz and Maximilian "Max" David Muñiz. At birth, Emme weighed approximately **5.5** pounds, and Max weighed **6** pounds. Angelina Jolie gave birth to twins on July 12, 2008, a boy, named Knox Leon, who weighed approximately **5** pounds and a girl, Vivienne, who also weighed **5** pounds. Tila Tequila weighs **98** pounds. 5.5 + 6 + 5 + 5 + 98 = 119.5. 119.5 + 300 = **419.5.** Paris Hilton has dated **2** Greek shipping heirs, Paris Latsis and Stavros Niarchos III. 419.5 divided by 2 = **209.75.** The amount of money that Hugh Grant paid Divine Brown for a blow job was **$50.** The amount of money that Eliot Spitzer paid Ashley

Alexandra Dupré for an hour's worth of sex was **$1,000.** 209.75 × 50/1000 = **10.4875.** There are **1,420** calories in a Hardee's Monster Thickburger. 1420 + 10.4875 = **1430.4875.** According to costumer James Taylor, actor Marlon Brando split the seat on **52** pairs of pants during the shooting of *Mutiny on the Bounty.* The square root of 52 is **7.2111.** 1430.4875 divided by 7.2111 = **198.37299.**

INTERNATIONAL BRAIN DAYS

If you want to try something a little "different" that sort of stretches the envelope of your brain and gives it an opportunity to move beyond its habitual day-to-day functions, designate certain days as International Brain Days. These are days in which you'll try to tax your mind in an unusual way. For instance,

• For an entire day, try expressing yourself exclusively in Doctor Speak: Instead of saying you're going to "make a doody," announce that you're off to attend a "lower gastrointestinal seminar where you plan to produce a significant amount of fecal matter." On your Brain Day, remember to "palpate" rather than "touch." Don't "stretch"—"dilate." Don't "touch," "poke," or "prod"—"palpate." And of course, never "spit" or "piss"—"expectorate" and "micturate."

• Combine two very disparate movies and—for a day—"channel" the hybrid character. For example:

● *A Beautiful Mind* and *Carrie:* Telekinetically levitate pieces of chalk that then scribble arcane equations on a blackboard, or as you're developing your own embedding theorems (which state that every Riemannian manifold can be isometrically embedded in a Euclidean space), have your friends dump a bucket of pig's blood over your head.

Or for something more medical . . .

● Patch Adams and *Silence of the Lambs:* When you play doctor with wife or girlfriend, you have a simultaneous desire to make her laugh and eat her liver with some fava beans and a nice chianti.

TIME TRAVEL: BACK . . . BACK . . . BACK . . .

You have no idea how much you have stored away in that mind of yours. There is a rich archive of memories—experiences, people, places, smells, sounds, etc. that you're not aware of. It's quite amazing what a treasure trove you have but never access.

Here's a little game you can play that will not only work out those memory-retrieval functions but that will also enable you to revisit times and places in your life that you thought had evaporated over all these years.

This exercise is called Time Travel and it's a totally cool mental "video game" you can play anywhere, anytime. And you don't need an Xbox or a PlayStation. Just your own brain.

Close your eyes and go back in time . . . back, back, back . . . to, say, the house you lived in when you were 15 years old. Open the door . . . you'll be blown away by what you can actually remember if you simply walk yourself through the house. . . .

There's that blue armoire that Mom used to keep the mail on . . . there are the steps going upstairs . . . hey, I'd forgotten all about that big chunk of the banister that was gouged out when we carried my sister's television upstairs that time . . . oh God . . . that weird fuzzy green carpet up at the top of the landing . . . there's my room . . . check out that groovy zebra-print wallpaper! . . .

OK, now here's the best part. This will truly amaze you. Pick a drawer in your old bedroom and open it up, that top one in your dresser—the one with all the miscellaneous stuff. You can do this! It's incredible. C'mon, just open it up in your mind. . . . It's all in your memory. . . . Now, look in the drawer, rummage around. . . .

There's a Bazooka Joe comic . . . smell it . . . it's got that great sweet pink aroma, right? . . . There's an Oranjeboom beer label. . . . There's that horseshoe my parents bought me at the blacksmith shop in Williamsburg, Virginia . . . a 1969 Joe Pepitone baseball card . . . an unopened Trojan condom . . . shit! There's that roach clip with the little turquoise-and-crystal dragonfly . . . that fancifully porno-graphic stick-figure drawing that Susan Poznak made for me on a pink Post-it of the two of us dangling from an iron trestle over the turbid waters of the Elbe River dividing East and West Germany with some cryptic caption, "He can't refuse." . . . There's a *TV Guide* . . . let's leaf through it for a moment and check out some of the shows . . . *Hawaii Five-0, Soul Train, Night Gallery, McMillan and Wife, Cannon* . . .

You gotta try this! Time Travel is guaranteed to leave you drenched in sweat, and with a bulging hippocam-pus like you've never seen!

AREN'T YOU FEELING SMARTER NOW?

Had you wanted to go to a "real" medical school, you would have had to have taken the Medical College Admission Test (MCAT), a standardized, multiple-choice examination designed to assess your problem solving, critical thinking, writing skills, and your knowl-edge of science concepts and principles prerequisite to the study of medicine. ZZZZZZZZZZZ . . . .

Please. After chapter 1 you are primed and ready to dissect your first cadaver.

CHAPTER 2

You want to know the truth? Studies have shown that doctors don't remember much of what they learn in the first two years of medical school. After only three months, they forget up to 20 percent of what they've studied, and if you ask most M.D.s, they'll tell you they remember almost nothing, especially when it comes to the anatomy

TALKING THE BODY TALK
Anatomy 101

class that you are forced to go through in your first year. So why put yourself through all those endless hours of painful cramming? You just need to focus on the important stuff.

Yeah, that's right. Do you think the mechanic at the service department of your Toyota dealership knows how to fix the suspension of a Jaguar? Does the cook at your favorite Chinese restaurant need to know how to make a perfect soufflé? Does it really matter to most docs that the arterial supply to the anal canal is from the superior and inferior rectal arteries? Of course not! And, believe me, your dermatologist certainly doesn't know squat about the meniscus of your knee. And why should he? As long as he knows how to tell a pimple from an insect bite, he can charge you $125 for looking at it. That's because he's got the vocabulary to work in his specialty. Our advice here is to focus on vocabulary. If you know the words to use, you don't actually have to know where the body parts are in order to act and sound like a doctor.

SO, WHAT PARTS OF THE HUMAN BODY DO YOU REALLY NEED TO KNOW?

The secret to sounding like a real M.D. is having a versatile repertoire of juicy tidbits of information about the body. Don't even try to learn everything. It's a colossal waste of time. A little knowledge goes a very long way. Remember, *less* is *more*. All it takes is one—that's right, *only one*—carefully deployed anatomical fact for you to achieve instant "I'm sort of like a doctor" credibility. And you can use that one fact over and over and over again.

Here's an EZ-to-use instant guide to how to work choice bits of "doctor-sounding" dialogue into your everyday life. . . . Skim this chapter as quickly as you can, and before you can say "pilonidal cyst," you'll be sounding like Mehmet freakin' Oz!

Here's an example: That squishy little pink thing at the inside corner of your eye is called the caruncula lachrymalis or the lachrymal caruncle. The surface of the caruncle contains sebaceous glands, hair follicles, and sweat gland elements. The function of the caruncula is unclear. The famous Renaissance anatomist Andreas Vesalius wrote in his book *On the Fabric of the Human Body (De Humani Corporis Fabrica)* that the caruncle "is said to have been created to prevent any phlegm purged from the brain into the eye sockets from flowing down onto the cheeks, but instead to fall completely through this foramen [ductus nasolacrimalis] into the space of the nostrils." The lachrymal caruncle is thought to be the source of the whitish secretion that constantly collects in this region (that would be "eye snot"). Enlarged lacrimal caruncles are called megalocaruncles. And, presumably, megalocaruncles produce mega-eye-snot.

OK. That's enough to get you started. (TALK ABOUT ZERO LEARNING CURVE!!) The mind boggles at the almost limitless opportunities you'll have to insinuate this fascinating and arcane piece of anatomical lore into your daily conversation. Try tossing even just a morsel into a random conversation at the supermarket checkout line, nail salon, or gym locker room. Then watch that look of deep, awestruck respect wash over the face of whomever you're talking to.

Wouldn't it have been great if Jack Nicholson had said to Helen Hunt, "You make me wanna be the sort of Renaissance man whose lacrimal caruncles prevent his brain phlegm from flowing down his cheeks," instead of the relatively insipid "You make me wanna be a better man" in that cheesy movie?

MEDICAL SCHOOL FLASHBACK

Be happy that you are avoiding my most penetrating memory from anatomy class, the overwhelming stench of formaldehyde. It saturates your skin, nostrils, and clothes. There is nothing worse than bringing that sandwich or slice of pizza to your mouth and getting a whiff of pickled human mixed with the soap you used to unsuccessfully purge the scent from your hands. Makes you want to puke just thinking about it. And you wonder why they call it Gross Anatomy.

—Dr. Billy

WE'D LIKE YOU TO MEET "BOB"

Bob's a nice, friendly guy. After falling in with the wrong crowd in his early twenties, and spending a couple of years in the joint, Bob's really turned his life around. Now all Bob wants to do is help people—always ready to offer a handy bench-press spot, volunteering to jump-start your car even though he's late to his appointment with his probation officer, that sort of thing.

We believe that everyone deserves a second chance. Because Bob is such an appealing and persuasive (one might even say sociopathic) fellow, we've hired him to work at the Why Do Men Have Nipples School of Medicine as one of our demonstration mentors.

Bob's going to help us show you how to work anatomical facts into everyday situations, so you'll be able to impress your family, friends, and coworkers, and sort of sound like a real doctor. Just read on to see how Bob uses his awesome doctor vocabulary to excellent effect.

Bob Lesson 1: At the Bar

BOB (singing along to the jukebox): "Hold me closer, Tony Danza / Count the headlights on the highway" . . . I love Elton John.

LAURA (not her real name): Excuse me?

BOB: Oh, I'm sorry. I didn't mean to bother you. I was just saying that I love Elton John.

LAURA: Me too.

BOB: You know, this might sound weird, but I think one of the reasons I admire Elton John so much is that he wears glasses. I have a lot of respect for people who don't go the whole contact lens/Lasik eye surgery route. It shows that they're not vain, that they're involved in more serious endeavors than being obsessed with superficial appearances. . . .

LAURA (unconsciously reaching up to touch her eyeglasses): Really? That's a very enlightened point of view.

BOB: I'm Bob, by the way.

LAURA: I'm Laura.

BOB: Laura . . . *enchanté.* What do you do?

LAURA: I'm a library systems coordinator at the Mendel Gottesman Library of Hebraica/Judaica at Yeshiva University.

BOB: Can I buy you a drink?

LAURA: I don't see why not.

BOB (to the bartender): Lloyd, two shots of Jack and a pair of Buds.

Bob suddenly grimaces, groans, and grabs his head with both hands.

LAURA: Are you all right?

BOB: I think so. . . . I think I'm feeling you deep in my dorsal caudate, and you're stimulating my ventral tegmental areas to pump out dopamine.

LAURA (coyly): I am?

BOB: Researchers using functional magnetic resonance imaging (fMRI) have found that intense romantic love is associated with activation occurring in the right ventral tegmental area (VTA) and dorsal caudate body. These regions are rich with dopamine, a naturally produced chemical that serves as a neurotransmitter in the brain, and the chemical most associated with . . . *l'amour.*

LAURA: Would you like to get out of here?

BOB: Is now soon enough? I live in an SRO near the bus station. How about your place?

LAURA (breathlessly): *Vamanos.*

CUT!

Bob's Vocab

Ventral—pertaining to the front or anterior of any structure. The ventral surfaces of the body include the chest, abdomen, shins, palms, and soles. The opposite of *ventral* is *dorsal*. (You should make sure to throw those terms around liberally!)

Ventral tegmental area (VTA)—located in the midbrain, at the top of the brainstem. The VTA, or the ventral tegmentum, is one of the most primitive parts of the brain.

Dorsal caudate body—a part of the brain located near the center, sitting aside the thalamus. There is a caudate within each hemisphere (half) of the brain. The caudate is an important part of the brain's learning and memory system. It has recently been found to be associated with falling in love.

HUMOR IS THE BEST MEDICINE

"God gave men both a penis and a brain,
but unfortunately not enough blood supply to run
both at the same time."

—Robin Williams

POP QUIZ Know Your Own Body

Which of the following is true?
A. A person can expect to breathe in about 40 pounds of dust over his/her lifetime.
B. One square inch of human skin contains 625 sweat glands.
C. It's impossible to sneeze with your eyes open.
D. The aorta, the largest artery in the body, is almost the diameter of a garden hose.

Answer: All of the above

True or False?
Dr. Henry Gray, world-renowned professor of anatomy and Fellow of the Royal Society, was inspired to go to medical school after working as

a summer intern as a production assistant on the set of TV's *Grey's Anatomy.*

Answer: False

Dr. Henry Gray (1827–1861) never had the pleasure of watching or working on this popular TV show (television wasn't invented until a hundred years after his birth by Philo Farnsworth in 1927). Without this distraction, Dr. Gray was able to focus on his studies and ultimately write the best-known and oldest textbook of anatomy in current use. That's right. *Gray's Anatomy* is actually a book! It was first published in 1858 under the title *Anatomy, Descriptive and Surgical.*

Bob Lesson 2: In the Bedroom

LAURA: Bob, don't you think that light you installed is a little bright?

BOB: That's a high-output 23-inch surgery light-head they use in operating rooms. It's a 150-watt tungsten halogen bulb with 102,000 lux at 1 meter. I want to see *everything*, Laura.

Laura slides off her Tweety Bird underpants.

BOB: I taut I taw a puddy tat.

LAURA: Yeah . . . talk dirty to me, Bob. It makes me *so* hot.

BOB: The average erect penis measures 5.5 to 6.2 inches long and has a circumference of 4.7 to 5.1 inches. The autonomic nervous system controls the innervation of the penis, specifically branches of the pudendal nerve, which are derived from spinal cord levels S2, S3, and S4.

LAURA: Yeah, baby . . . tell me more.

BOB: The muscle which withdraws the testicle into the body when exposed to cold is the cremaster. In males, the cremasteric reflex can be elicited by stroking the superior and medial part of the thigh in a downward direction. The normal response in males is a contraction of the muscle that pulls up the scrotum and testes on the side that is being stroked. In lay terms, Laura, you scratch the inner thigh and the balls rise! In females, the muscle fibers are incorporated into the round ligament which helps suspend the uterus.

LAURA: Oh, Bob . . . that's so good.

BOB: On October 9, 1562, the esteemed Italian anatomist and physician Gabrielo Falloppio died, at the age of only thirty-nine. He is the namesake of the Fallopian tubes—the two tubes leading from the ovaries to the uterus—which he first identified. The aqueductus Fallopii, the canal through which the facial nerve passes after leaving the auditory nerve, is also named after him. Falloppio, a professor of anatomy at Ferrara, Pisa, and the University of Padua, inaugurated many anatomical terms, naming the cochlea, the placenta, the vagina, and the clitoris.

LAURA: Oh, yeah . . . don't stop. Please don't stop!

BOB: Dr. Francois Gigot de la Peyronie was physician to King Louis XV of France. Not a bad gig, but not what he's famous for. In 1743, Dr. Peyronie first described the affliction that's named after him: Peyronie's disease, a condition in which the penis becomes crooked when erect. The cause is a plaque or thickening of fibrous tissue on one side of the penis which causes it to bend or arc. Peyronie's disease occurs in about one in one hundred men. Many researchers believe that the plaque of Peyronie's disease develops following penile trauma (hitting or bending) that causes localized bleeding inside the penis.

LAURA: Yes, just like that, just like that . . . more historical/sexual esoterica . . . give it to me!

BOB: Although many historians have long contended that Louis XVI and his bride, Marie Antoinette, had trouble in the boudoir because Louis was either impotent or suffered from a phimosis, the royal couple's inability to conceive children was actually the result of the fact that Marie Antoinette's unusually thick hymen painfully resisted penetration. After a relatively minor surgical procedure, everything was *très bien*, and in due time, the queen gave birth to their first child, Marie-Thérésé-Charlotte.

LAURA: Oh God . . . I'm coming, Bob!!!! This has never happened to me before! I'm squirting!!!! It's your encyclopedic command of medical knowledge!

CUT!

Bob's Vocab
Phimosis—a medical condition in which the foreskin of the penis cannot be fully retracted.

Cochlea—a spiral-shaped tube in the inner ear and the main organ of hearing. The cochlea contains the nerve endings that transmit sound vibrations from the middle ear to the auditory nerve.

POP QUIZ Know Your Own Body

Which of the following is false?

A. There are 206 bones in the human body.
B. Adults have 32 teeth, including wisdom teeth.
C. The human small bowel is about 40 feet long.
D. The average red blood cell lives for 120 days.

Answer: C; the human small bowel is about 20 feet long.

Which of the following is false?

A. There are 2.5 trillion (give or take) red blood cells in your body at any moment.
B. Nerve impulses travel at over 400 kilometers per hour (250 mi/hr).

C. A cough moves out at 100 kilometers per hour (60 mi/hr).

D. Our heart beats around 500,000 times every day.

Answer: D; our heart beats around 100,000 times every day.

Which of the following is false?

A. We make 3 liters of saliva a day.

B. A red blood cell can circumnavigate your body in less than 20 seconds.

C. A sneeze generates a wind of 166 kilometers per hour (103 mi/hr).

D. We are about 70 percent water.

Answer: A; we make 1 liter of saliva a day.

LET'S PLAY DOCTOR MISCELLANY

Do Blondes Have More Hair?

Remember that saying that "Blondes have more fun"? Well, that is just speculation, but it does seem that blond people generally have more hair on their scalps than people with other hues. Blond people have about 150,000 hairs on their heads, edging out the brunettes by about 40,000 hairs.

Brown-haired people: 110,000 hairs
Black-haired people: 100,000 hairs
Red-haired people: 90,000 hairs

Completely Random Hair Fact

Our entire body is covered with hair except for our lips, palms of the hands, and soles of the feet.

What's the fastest-growing hair on your body?

Right now, about 90 percent of your hair is growing and about 10 percent is resting. After growing for up to 5 years, a hair will go into a resting phase for up to 12 weeks. After that resting phase, the hair falls out and a new hair starts to grow. You could be losing up to 100 scalp hairs per day.

When you're developing inside your mom's uterus,

all of your hair follicles are formed by week 22. That's a total of five million follicles all over the body. One million of those are on the head, and 100,000 are on the scalp. And that's the most you will ever have. From that point on, it's all downhill.

As for speed, the Head Hair is the Road Runner of all hairs (but just by a hair).

Oh, by the way, we have about 600 eyebrow hairs and 420 eyelashes.

Approximate rate of hair growth:

Head hair: .35 millimeters per day
Facial hair: .30 millimeters per day
Underarm hair: .30 millimeters per day
Pubic hair: .20 millimeters per day
Eyebrows: .16 millimeters per day

Bob Lesson 3: At the Dentist's Office

DENTAL HYGIENIST: OK, Bob, I just want you to gently bite down on the plastic holder here so we can take a couple of X-rays. . . .

BOB: Did you know that the adult mouth contains thirty-two permanent teeth?

DENTAL HYGIENIST: Yes, I know that. I'm a dental hygienist.

BOB: And that the cuspids or canine teeth of the upper jaw are also called the eyeteeth. And they're called eyeteeth because they sit directly under the eyes. It's also thought that this name comes from the Renaissance anatomist Galen, who thought that a nerve in these teeth came from a nerve that also supplied the eye. Turns out Galen was wrong when he stated that "the eye, the instrument of vision, is hidden in the cavity above, and in that below is the humor which nourishes the roots of the teeth."

DENTAL HYGIENIST: That's very interesting, Bob. Now, if you don't mind, just open wide and bite down on the holder. . . .

BOB: Did you know that Mao Zedong never brushed his teeth? He just washed his mouth out in the morning with tea. His teeth were coated with a green patina. And when his doctor suggested to him that he should use a toothbrush, do you know what Mao's reply was? Mao said: "A tiger never brushes his teeth."

DENTAL HYGIENIST: I wasn't aware of that.

BOB: Did you know that Clark Gable had false teeth and legendary bad breath?

DENTAL HYGIENIST: No, I didn't know that.

BOB (incredulous): You didn't know that Clark Gable had bad breath—legendary bad breath?

DENTAL HYGIENIST: No.

BOB: And you call yourself a dental hygienist?

The dental hygienist slumps with shame.

BOB: Hand over your lead apron.

DENTAL HYGIENIST: What?

BOB: You don't deserve to wear the coveted lead apron. The lead apron is reserved exclusively for those who have mastered the arcane lore of dental hygiene.

With abject humiliation, she removes the lead apron.

Bob, the plastic X-ray film holder jutting jauntily from the corner of his mouth, dons the lead apron and strides out of the office.

CUT!

POP QUIZ Know Your Own Body

Which of the following is false?

A. Our lungs inhale more than two million liters of air every day.

B. Our nose is our personal air-conditioning system: It warms cold air, cools hot air, and filters impurities.

C. It is believed that the main purpose of eyebrows is to keep sweat out of the eyes.

D. The longest muscle in our body is the quadriceps.

Answer: D; the longest muscle in our body is the sartorius. It is a straplike, narrow muscle that runs from the hip to the knee.

Which of the following is true?

A. Almost 80 percent of the people in the United States wear eyeglasses.

B. The total spent for eyeglasses in the United States is around $5 billion.

C. Each of the eyeballs is moved by four muscles.

D. The retina is the only part of the central nervous system that can be seen from outside of the body . . . you have to look through the pupil of the eye to see it.

Answer: D; 50 percent of people wear eyeglasses, we spend $13 billion on eyeglasses, and each of the eyeballs is moved by six muscles.

LET'S PLAY DOCTOR MISCELLANY

How many times do you blink per day?
The average person blinks approximately 15 times per minute. If you're awake for 16 hours a day, that's a grand total of 14,400 blinks a day. A blink takes about 300 to 400 milliseconds—that's 3/10ths to 4/10ths of a second. So you're probably spending more than an hour a day just blinking! No wonder life seems so hectic, huh?! Excessive blinking of both eyes is called blepharospasm, from the Greek word for eyelid, *blepharon.* (In case you're curious, the band Blink 182—which in 2000 released a behind-the-scenes DVD titled *The Urethra Chronicles*—is on "indefinite hiatus.")

What is saliva actually made of?

Ninety-eight percent water. (Boring, right? Isn't almost everything 98 percent water? Beer, white clam sauce, Jessica Simpson . . . it's all about 98 percent water.) Saliva also contains electrolytes, mucus, and various enzymes (e.g., amylase). Our salivary glands produce about 2 to 4 pints of drool a day.

Speaking of pints . . . the Jivaro Indians of the Ecuadorian Amazon prepare a beer made out of manioc tubers. And it's the Jivaro women who are the brewmeisters, chewing handfuls of manioc mash and spitting them back into the pot. Mastication of the mash is considered essential to the brewing process, and scientists opine that it's the enzymes in the saliva that hasten the fermentation. Jivaro men opine that the beer is better if it's been chewed by a pretty girl rather than an old woman. So whether the demographic is Jivaro guys in the Amazon or frat boys in Daytona, the content of the beer commercial is pretty much the same: Saliva of the Fittest.

Bob Lesson 4: At a Downtown Poetry Reading

Downtown Poet in dark Ray-Bans, a filthy Fruit Loops T-shirt, and torn black jeans steps up to the microphone.

DOWNTOWN POET: I'd like to dedicate this poem to my mother, who was never there when I needed her:

> The Black Death, The Spanish Inquisition, The
>   Rape of Nanking
> Mother, where are you?
> Mother, I can't see you.
>
> Wounded Knee, Babi Yar, Hiroshima, Nagasaki,
>   Rwanda
> Mom, please . . . I need you.
> Mom, please call.
>
> Speck, Gacy, Bundy, Manson, Pol Pot
> Mommy, I'm really upset . . . I need money.
>
> Jonestown, Columbine, Bhopal, Chernobyl
> Mommy . . . hold me.
> Mommy . . . I'm really hungry.
> Mommy, make me macaroni and cheese.
>
> Momma . . . Momma . . . Momma . . .
> Momma.

The audience applauds.

Now Bob, wearing a lead apron and khaki Dockers, steps up to the mike.

BOB: I am Bob. I would like to recite some classic medical school anatomic verse to remember the arduous course that the lingual nerve takes as it weaves its way from the jaw to the tongue:

> The Lingual nerve
> Took a curve
> Around the Hyoglossus.
> "Well I'll be fucked!"
> Said Wharton's Duct,
> "The bastard's gone and crossed us!"

CUT!

Bob's Vocab

Lingual nerve—a branch of the mandibular nerve, itself a branch of the trigeminal nerve (one of the cranial nerves), that provides sensation to the floor of the mouth and the anterior two-thirds of the tongue.

Want to show off how you remember the cranial nerves? Use this medical mnemonic: **O**n **O**ld **O**lympus **T**owering **T**ops, **A** **F**at-**A**ss **G**erman **V**iewed **S**ome **H**ops (I-**O**ptic, II-**O**lfactory, III-**O**culomotor, IV-**T**rochlear, V-**T**rigeminal, VI-**A**bducens, VII-**F**acial, VIII-**A**coustic (vestibulocochlear), IX-**G**lossopharyngeal, X-**V**agus, XI-**S**pinal accessory, XII-**H**ypoglossal).

Hyoglossus—a flat muscle on each side of the tongue connecting it with the hyoid bone. The hyoglossus depresses and retracts the tongue.

Wharton's duct—the duct of the submandibular salivary gland opening into the mouth below the tongue.

POP QUIZ Know Your Own Body

Which of the following is false?

A. A completely full bladder is capable of holding approximately 1 liter of fluid (the urge to urinate occurs when the bladder contains about 200 ml of urine).

B. The eyeball is about 1 inch (2.5 cm) in diameter.

C. The human esophagus is about 10 inches (25 cm) long.

D. An adult human brain has more than one billion neurons.

Answer: D; an adult human brain has more than 100 billion neurons.

Which of the following is true?

The tiniest muscle, the stapedius of the middle ear, is just 1/5 of an inch long.

The average human head weighs about 10 pounds.

The average human brain weighs about 3 pounds

A fetus acquires fingerprints at the age of three months.

Answer: All of the above

HUMOR IS THE BEST MEDICINE

"After two days in hospital, I took a turn for the nurse."

—W. C. Fields

LET'S PLAY DOCTOR MISCELLANY

Veterinary Anatomy

It always helps to be able to wow your friends with obscure anatomical ditties about our animal friends.

You may be interested in which creature is the most well endowed in the world. Without a doubt, the blue whale is the Tommy Lee of the animal kingdom—

its penis is 11 feet long, and its testicles weigh up to 100 pounds each.

Did you know that Aristotle Onassis upholstered the bar stools on his yacht *Christina* with whale penis leather?

Traveling to Iceland? Don't miss the the Icelandic Phallological Museum! It's devoted entirely to the study of animal penises. This cultural destination is located in the Húsavíkurbær municipality in the northern part of Iceland and contains a collection of more than 150 penises and penile parts belonging to almost all the land and sea mammals that can be found in Iceland.

Bob Lesson 5: At the Airport

Bob is trying to pass through security.

TSA AGENT: Boarding pass?

BOB: I don't have a boarding pass, TSA Agent . . . (he checks the agent's name tag). . . . TSA Agent *Baljeet*. But I think this should suffice.

Bob flashes his Why Do Men Have Nipples School of Medicine Universal Boarding Pass (which is to air travel what M.D. plates are to parking).

TSA AGENT: Very good, sir. Now, I'm going to need you to place all metallic objects in that bin and kindly remove your shoes.

BOB: No problem, bro, but what about the socks? I'm wearing sock garters. I had a bad long-jumping accident at the Olympiastadion in Munich—pulled a 9.1 meters, world record, but they invalidated it because of excessive wind speed. Tore my calf muscles. The two main muscles are the soleus and the gastrocnemius. Tore 'em both, dude. Socks just wouldn't stay up after that.

TSA AGENT: Sir, I appreciate the anatomy lesson, but let's keep moving. Leave the socks and we can wand you if we have to.

BOB (walking through the metal detector): Oooooh . . . I've never been wanded before by a man in uniform. This is all turning into an *Oz* episode. (He beeps.)

TSA AGENT: Sir, please spread your arms and legs.

BOB: How about if I just drop my pants, bend over, and you and your sadistic fraternity brothers can just sodomize me right here. (He winks at the TSA Agent, then turns to the crowded queues of agitated passengers behind him.) Hey, everybody—it's Happy Hour at Alpha Kappa Pi!

Bob beeps again as the agent moves the wand across his chest.

TSA AGENT (pointing to Bob's chest): What's *that?!*

BOB: Relax, it's just an extra nipple. I'm a polytheliac. You got a problem with that? *Polythelia* is the fancy word for the condition of having more than the regular number of nipples. These accessory nipples or supernumerary nipples usually occur in a line below the existing nipple. They call it the nipple line or the mammary ridge. Doesn't *mammary ridge* sound like a vacation spot? People often don't know that they have the triple nipple because they can be small and often are mistaken for birthmarks or moles. Also, they're more commonly found in men, so don't pick up your girlfriend's shirt looking for extras—you'll be disappointed.

Bob leaps up onto the security conveyor belt and flexes his arms.

BOB: You ever see a pair of guns like this in your life? Battleships, bro! You know the biceps are actually called *biceps brachii*. It is given the name *biceps* because it has two heads. Contrary to popular belief, it's not the main flexor of the forearm. That's the *brachialis* muscle.

Bob goes into full pose-down mode with a Twisted Crunch—the forward arm tucked behind the head, showing off the serratus and intercostals muscles. He then pops a Crab—the Incredible Hulk pose—arms forward and down, making an arch in front of the body, fists clenched over the stomach, the traps pulled up and the chest flexed. Half a dozen security agents, brandishing Tasers, rush Bob, knocking him off the conveyor belt.

Later, seated in the First Class Lounge, sipping martinis with the very agents who Tased him . . .

BOB: The presence of more than two testicles is called polyorchidism. It's extremely rare. In fact, less than a hundred cases have been reported in the literature. Three balls—triorchidism—is the most common presentation. . . . Dude, you gonna eat your olives?

CUT!

Bob's Vocab

Soleus, gastrocnemius, biceps brachii, serratus, intercostals—These are just muscles. Any physical therapist or massage therapist could tell you this. To be a Real Fake Doc, you need an obscure term for a common thing like the following:

Natal cleft—the groove between the buttocks that runs from below the sacrum to the perineum; or the groove in which the anus is situated. Yes, it's the ass crack.

MEDICAL SCHOOL FLASHBACK

Trauma codes were always the best part of my third-year surgery rotation. Our team would get the call that EMS was on its way with a car accident victim (an "MVC" [Motor Vehicle Collision] in doctor lingo), or someone hit by a car (a "pedestrian [ped] struck") or a bullet (a "GSW" [Gun Shot Wound]). We—the medical student, intern, resident, and chief resident—would run down the stairwell to the ER, our white coats flapping behind us like superhero capes. Once there, we would put on blue plastic gowns with matching booties and poorly fitting latex-free gloves that would start to stick to our sweaty hands as we waited with anticipation for the ambulance to hit the door.

I felt this sense of excitement even though the main role of medical students in a trauma was to stand at the foot of the bed and feel for pulses in the patient's feet. Our other main task was to fetch warm sheets to cover the fully exposed patient. Sometimes our residents would throw us a bone in the form of the Foley catheterization. This meant that we got to place a plastic tube into the patient's urethra, which would stay there to collect urine. It was as close to performing a minor surgery as we got.

My very first Foley catheterization during a trauma was on a woman who had been in a car accident. I prepared her genital area sterilely and began to insert the catheter. "Ouch!" screamed the patient as my catheter hit resistance. I tried again—"Ooow!" And again. I felt sweat dripping down my neck as I thought frantically about why I could not get the catheter to pass through the urethra. After fifteen minutes of struggle I heard giggling from my senior teammates, who were watching me from behind. "Try a little lower, unless you want to keep trying to catheterize this lady's clitoris," my senior resident suggested while laughing. I never lived that moment down, and for the rest of my rotation my team reminded me often of my attempt at clitoral catheterization.

—Dr. Kelly Doran, emergency medicine resident

POP QUIZ Know Your Own Body

Which of the following is false?

A. Capillaries are so small that it takes ten of them to equal the thickness of a human hair.

B. Your body has about 5.6 liters (6 qts) of blood.

C. Babies start dreaming even before they're born.

D. The skull is composed of nine different bones.

Answer: D; the skull is composed of twenty-nine different bones.

Bob Lesson 6: In the Men's Room

Bob is sitting in the stall in the airport bathroom.

BOB (he moves his foot to get the attention of the guy next door): Don't get the wrong idea. Just wondering if you had any idea how much pee my bladder can hold?

TRAVELER: (no answer . . . just a groan)

BOB: I didn't think so. The bladder can hold about twelve to sixteen ounces of urine. When your bladder contains about eight to ten ounces of urine, you will normally feel the urge to urinate.

A full bladder is roughly the size of a softball.
(Bob reaches his hand under the stall.) Hi! I'm Bob.

TRAVELER: (He shakes Bob's hand, but no answer . . . another groan.)

BOB: Sounds like you're struggling there, partner. You're not alone. A study published in 2006 looked at the Direct Medical Costs of Constipation in the United States. Researchers found that constipation was a diagnosis or a reason for seeking care in 5.7 million outpatient (ambulatory) visits. When combining an additional 38,000 inpatient visits, the price tag for treating constipation was $235 million per year.

TRAVELER: (another groan) No shit!

BOB: My point exactly!

CUT!

POP QUIZ Know Your Own Body

Which of the following is true?

A. Nerve impulses move at approximately 100 meters per second.

B. Humans have more than 600 muscles.

C. The longest bone in the body is the humerus in the arm.

D. Your skin surface is completely replaced four times a year.

Answer: A and B; your skin surface is replaced once a month, and the longest bone is the femur.

Livin' La Vida Doctor

Writing the Perfect Get Out of Work Note (Beginner)

To Whom It May Concern:

Mr. _____ was seen in my office for the incision and drainage of an infected pilonidal cyst. The cyst cavity was opened and marsupialized. Mr. _____ was discharged in good condition with a strict regimen of sitz baths, antibiotics, and dressing changes. He may have difficulty sitting for prolonged periods and should be encouraged to take long, relaxing walks. Pilonidal cysts can be extremely painful and Mr. _____ was prescribed narcotic analgesics. Despite his reluctance to take mind-altering substances during the workday, I insist that he adhere to my pain-control regime.

Dr. _____

Dept. of Surgery

Memorial Hospital

LET'S PLAY DOCTOR MISCELLANY

What does it mean to be *double-jointed* ?

Double-jointedness doesn't actually mean having two joints where there would normally be one. *Double-jointed* is a popular term used to describe a joint that is unusually flexible or that stretches farther than normal. Doctors use the terms *hyperflexible, hyperextensible,* or, most frequently, *hypermobile*. Some people who are hypermobile can, for example, bend their thumbs all the way back to their wrists. Since hypermobility seems to run in families, it's thought that there's a genetic component to the condition.

Why do so many older people break their hips?

More than 90 percent of hip fractures occur in older people with osteoporosis, a loss of bony tissue resulting in brittle bones that are more liable to fracture. This is an extremely serious health problem for our elderly. Unfortunately, almost 30 percent of older people who break a hip die within a year. (This is according to research conducted by the University of Maryland School of Medicine.) Each year, approximately 300,000 Americans over the age of 64 break their hips—75 percent of them women. Women are at higher risk than men because of the effects of menopause and the subsequent estrogen deficiency which can cause women to lose about 1 percent of their bone density in each ensuing year after menopause.

Bob Lesson 7: At the Dinner Table (with your prospective in-laws)

Cedar Rapids, Iowa.

BOB: These sweetbreads are absolutely delicious! What a contrast to the disgusting, insipid airline "cuisine" I've had to put up with.

LAURA'S MOM: Why, thank you, Bob. We're so glad you were able to take time out from your hectic schedule and pay us a visit.

LAURA (beaming, eager to show off her fiancé's medical erudition): Bob, sweetheart, what are sweetbreads actually?

LAURA'S MOM: Oh, honey, even I know that. It's the pancreas of some poor animal.

BOB (makes a game-show buzz): Only partially correct, ma'am. Sweetbreads are most commonly made from the thymus gland of a young animal but also can be made from the pancreas. A calf or lamb is usually the "organ donor," and calves' sweetbreads are considered to be superior. Wanna know how to tell the difference? Thymus sweetbreads are elongated and irregular in shape, while pancreas sweetbreads are larger and rounded.

LAURA'S DAD: Who eats the guts, anyway? I'll have a steak, well done.

BOB (oblivious): You might be wondering: What is the thymus and what are its functions? The thymus is a small organ in your upper front chest, under your breastbone. Before birth and during childhood, the thymus helps the body make a type of white blood cell, the T cell. These cells help protect you from infections. The thymus continues to grow between birth and puberty and then begins to atrophy.

LAURA: You see, Mom, I told you. He knows everything.

LAURA'S DAD: I'm impressed. Where'd you get all this information anyway, boy?

BOB: I'm a demonstration mentor at the Why Do Men Have Nipples School of Medicine. Professors Goldberg and Leyner have developed a revolutionary pedagogical method that enables people to instantly sound like doctors without attending a day of medical school. Did you know that humans have 9,000 taste buds? Goats and pigs have 15,000, rabbits have 17,000, cattle have 25,000, and sharks have 100,000. Snakes have none.

LAURA: Daddy . . . Bob and I were hoping that, as a wedding gift, you might want to make a fairly sizable contribution to the school—an endowment. They'll name a wing after you.

LAURA'S MOM: Bob, I couldn't be happier that you've chosen my daughter. I'd like to propose a toast.

LAURA'S DAD: (puts two fingers in his mouth and produces an ear splitting whistle): Wait one goddamn minute here! Last I looked, I was still the head of this family. Cultural mores may have changed since I courted my wife, but I'd like to think that a man still has some minimal input into his daughter's future.

BOB: I couldn't agree more. But, sir, in some ancient cultures, the mother had a stronger role. In ancient Egyptian culture, a suitor sometimes used a female go-between to approach the girl's mother rather than her father. Then again, legend also has it that the ancient Egyptians were inspired by the sacred bird, the ibis, which practices colonic irrigation by filling its curved beak with water and inserting it into its anus to flush out decaying matter. The first known proctologist was an ancient Egyptian physician named Iri. Among his many honorific titles were "Shepherd of the Anus," "Keeper of the Bottom," and "Keeper of the Royal Rectum." It's possible that the first people to use the rectal route for introducing nutrients were the Mongols. They were reported to have used a cow's horn attached to an animal bladder that was filled with "nutritious fluid." This was inserted into the rectum and the result . . . one happy, healthy Mongol! Anyway, sir, I respect your traditions and I will honor your decision.

LAURA'S DAD (he looks at his wife, then at his daughter, and finally at Bob): Welcome to the family . . . Son. Who do I make that check out to? To the institute or to the two Jew doctors?

CUT!

LET'S PLAY DOCTOR MISCELLANY

Is everyone's normal temperature 98.6?

The body temperature 98.6 degrees Fahrenheit is actually an average. Your body's normal temperature can vary up or down by a full degree. Also, your temperature can change over the course of a day by a degree, depending on what activities you're engaged in and the time of day. Body temperature can also be acutely responsive to hormone levels and may rise or fall when a woman is ovulating or having her menstrual period. If you're very bored (and remember: only boring people get bored), take your temperature at various times of the day and month and chart your unique variations. Keep in mind that rectal or ear temperature readings are usually .5 to 1 degree Fahrenheit higher than oral readings.

CHAPTER 3

So, you've already read 93 pages. How does it feel to be well on your way to becoming a pseudodoctor? Pseudoawesome, right?

In "real" medical school, you have to sit through hours of tedious lectures during the first two years. Here at the Why Do Men Have Nipples School of Medicine, you can just sit on the toilet and cover all the important points of the classroom learning

DIAGNOSE THIS!
Acne or Leprosy — You Make the Call

process. The last chapter allowed you to essentially complete year one without enduring the rigors of all sorts of basic science courses such as Anatomy, Physiology, Histology, Biochemistry, Embryology, and Neuroanatomy. Now you're ready to move on to year two.

The second year places more emphasis on disease and its treatment. Courses include Pathology, Pharmacology, Pathophysiology, and Immunology. Again, it's tough going and requires enormous expenditures of time and effort. At the Why Do Men Have Nipples School of Medicine, the concepts of "time" and "effort" don't even exist! Just read on . . . and you'll be ready to start diagnosing patients instantly!

DIAGNOSE THIS

Sitting in your exam room is a 42-year-old man, reading Goethe's *Faust* in the original German. The patient complains of pain in his groin, especially when bending over and lifting, and also an uncomfortable sensation in the same area, which he describes as a "heavy, dragging feeling." When he stands upright, you notice a significant bulge in his lower abdomen.

Your diagnosis, Herr Doktor?

Answer: That bulge is the protruding intestine that results from an inguinal hernia. Just to make sure (and to impress the guy with your erudition and formidable linguistic skills), toss off something witty about selling one's soul to the devil, snap on your latex glove, place a finger at the top of his scrotum, and say: "*Drehen sie* *ihren kopf und husten.*" That means: Turn your head and cough.

DIAGNOSE THIS

Your patient, a backpacking hippie chick wearing a peasant blouse and Birkenstocks, presents with the following symptoms:

• Severe and continuous itching, especially at night

• Small red and crusty lesions that resemble pimples between her buttocks and under her breasts

• S-shaped burrows visible under the skin

She thinks her condition may be the result of an angry ex-boyfriend (a commodities trader, believe it or not) spiking her chai with nonorganic milk from hormone-riddled cows. What's she actually got?

Answer: You might want to confirm your diagnosis by doing a microscopic examination of a skin scraping to check for the mite or its eggs, but it sounds like scabies to me. Gently suggest to her that crystals and wheatgrass shots probably won't have much of an effect on the itching. Prescribe some permethrin cream (a skin cream to kill those critters), tell her to avoid fleabag hotels and dirty hostels, and send her on her way. Peace.

Livin' La Vida Doctor

Writing the Perfect Get Out of Work Note (Intermediate)

To Whom It May Concern:

_____ was seen in our emergency room on Nov. 23, 2006. He presented to the ER with severe muscle cramps, a rigid abdomen, and tachycardia. After a thorough nondiagnostic work-up for his acute abdominal pain, we discovered that he'd just returned from a weekend in western Texas where he'd been visiting his elderly grandma who was feeling lonely. While helping the recently widowed octogenarian clean out her toolshed, he must have suffered a *Latrodectus mactans* (black-widow spider) bite. Mr. _____ was promptly treated with narcotics and latrodectus antivenin. His symptoms responded remarkably well, confirming our diagnosis. Fatigue, weakness, and other nonspecific symptoms may persist for 7–10 days, but then Mr. _____ should make a complete recovery with no significant sequelae. Please excuse him from work during this difficult period. When Mr. _____ does return to work, it is imperative, in my medical opinion, that he be given great leeway in his arrival and departure times (due to residual fatigue from the antivenin treatment).

Sincerely,

Dr. _____

Dept. of Emergency Medicine, Our Lady of Mercy Hospital

DIAGNOSE THIS

You're doing your ER rotation, when a 35-year-old Chinese man is brought in by ambulance.

A large meat cleaver is embedded in the front of his skull. He's awake and talkative. Your supervising resident is busy with another trauma and sends you over to do an initial assessment. You've been studying hard and watching many episodes of *House*, so you jump at the chance. After a thorough history and physical, your resident returns and you're ready to impress him.

You state proudly, "I believe this man is suffering from acute West Nile encephalitis. During an episode of febrile delirium, he mistook his own head for a Peking duck. I think he needs a lumbar puncture and an infectious disease consult."

Your resident smacks you firmly in the back of the head and says, "When you hear hoofbeats, Einstein, think horses, not zebras. Dude's got a cleaver in his cranium. That's it. We're done here."

Now that you're a member of the medical community, you need to know this oft-repeated quote. In medical parlance, the term *zebra* is commonly used to refer to a rare disease or condition. Doctors are taught that the simplest or most obvious explanation is usually correct.

DIAGNOSE THIS

Your patient starts with a runny nose; red, watery eyes; mild fever; and a dry cough. . . . In about a week or two, he returns with worsening symptoms and now has episodic, severe coughing attacks and extreme fatigue. The cough is described as ending with a high-pitched sound as you gasp for air.

Answer: Whooping cough (pertussis). Next time remember to update the patient's vaccine and avoid this altogether!

DIAGNOSE THIS

Your patient has a headache and cramping of the jaw muscles. The next symptoms to present are difficulty swallowing, irritability, and spasms in the neck, arms, legs, and stomach. They may even get risus sardonicus, the appearance of a painful grin on your face due to facial muscle spasm. Untreated, next come spasms of the respiratory muscles that could lead to asphyxia.

Answer: Duh, they have tetanus.

What is so dangerous about a rusty nail?
Not that dangerous, especially if you drink in moderation. The most common recipe is 1½ ounces Scotch, ½ ounce Drambuie, and 1 twist of lemon peel. Allergic reactions to Drambuie (a honey- and herb-flavored golden scotch whisky liqueur) or lemon are uncommon, so . . . Oh, you mean if you step on one!

For some reason, rusty nails have also been thought to be a common source of tetanus. Tetanus is a serious disease that affects the nervous system, caused by the bacterium *Clostridium tetani*. Tetanus bacteria live in soil, saliva, dust, and manure and usually enter the body through a deep cut. Worldwide, tetanus is extremely common, estimated to affect nearly one million individuals every year. In the United States, there are only about 50 to 100 cases annually. These tend to occur in the elderly, intravenous drug users, and those who have never received the tetanus vaccine.

There is nothing special about the rusty nail that leads to tetanus. It is just that things tend to rust from being outside and therefore might be contaminated with the tetanus bacteria. Don't worry . . . just remember to get your vaccine.

DIAGNOSE THIS

Your patient just returned from a romantic vacation to South America. He and his lovely did some skinny-dipping in the Amazon and Oranoco Rivers. He presents with severe pain and bleeding while urinating. Budding urologists, travel medicine experts, and ichthyologists should have a good idea.

What ails him?

Answer: After ruling out a kidney stone, urine infection, and prostate infection, you must beware of the candirú (*Vandellia cirrhosa*), a 4- to 8-cm parasitic catfish indigenous to the Amazon River. Also known as the vampire fish of Brazil, this devilish little South American catfish has a healthy appetite for blood and has been known to swim into the urethra of urinating mammals (yes, that means your patient). Your patient must have urinated in the water, and the little guy just swam on in.

After the fish enters the urethra at high speed, the candirú clings tightly to the wall with spines that grow from its gills and upper jaw. Get the operating room ready, because only open urethrotomy (surgical incision of a stricture of the urethra) reliably removes the candirú.

If you are in the Amazon wilderness and don't want to perform self-surgery, you could try a local remedy. Get a local to help you find a jagua tree (*Genipa americana*), also called buitach apple. Pick the green fruit and drink the juice of the fruit as hot tea. The buitach apple contains large quantities of citric acid, which might dissolve the fish skeleton. Good luck.

DIAGNOSE THIS

When you come home from work, your roommate is curled up on the couch clutching his belly. That morning he had complained of some vague pain around his belly button and a loss of appetite. During the day he vomited and now he has a fever and severe pain on his right lower side. After you take advantage of his illness and finish his share of the leftover kung pao chicken, you amaze him with your diagnostic acumen.

What do you tell him?

Answer: That dude has the classic symptoms of acute appendicitis. Yes, periumbilical (pain around the belly button) pain followed by brief nausea, vomiting, and anorexia. After a few hours, the pain shifts to the right lower quadrant. Show him how smart you are by pointing to McBurney's point, a point one-third of the way along a line from the right hip to the navel. He should have severe pain if you press right there. Get him to the ER so he can get his appendix removed, or read chapter 4 and do it yourself.

DIAGNOSE THIS

You are working in the ER and a burly bouncer comes in with a big, red, swollen hand. He has a tiny cut over one of his middle knuckles. He says he was helping out behind the bar and cut his hand on a broken glass. So, Sherlock, what's the diagnosis?

Answer: Don't believe the brute. He probably has a clenched-fist injury. Ask him if it was a glass or if maybe he punched someone in the mouth. Clenched-fist injuries occur when a closed fist hits the teeth of another individual. The mouth is a dirty place and the tooth carries bacteria into the hand when it breaks the skin. Bacteria can enter the joint or track along the tendons, resulting in a serious condition. Get an X-ray to make sure there isn't a fracture, give antibiotics, call the hand surgeon, and recommend anger management.

MEDICAL SCHOOL FLASHBACK
Dressing the Part. . . .

During your first two years of medical school, you spent almost all of your time in the classroom. One exception for me was my physical diagnosis class. For this, a senior doctor would take all the wide-eyed medical students into the hospital to examine "real" patients. The first day was a harrowing experience. I prepared myself carefully. First I put on a clean, crisp shirt and a tie to make myself look professional. Then I added my new short white coat (the real doctors get the long white coats) and I stuffed the pockets with all of my newly purchased medical tools. I decided that it would be best to embark on this day with a full stomach, so I went to the cafeteria. Let's just say my stomach was a bit nervous, so I soon found myself sitting on a nearby toilet.

When I finished my business, I was ready to take on the world. I bent down to pick up my pants, but I guess I wasn't used to wearing a tie, as it found its way into the depths of the bowl. When I stood up, there was a waterline halfway up the tie like an oil dipstick. Looking much less professional (luckily I had already flushed) and without time to change, I buttoned up my white coat and went off to the hospital. This is how I began my illustrious medical career.

—Dr. Billy

DIAGNOSE THIS

You are examining a homeless patient who has a fever.
When you look in his mouth, you are almost knocked
over by the smell of his breath. He has marked swelling
of his gums, with small ulcerations that have a grayish
coloring. He tells you that his gums bleed easily. You are
almost a doctor, so you can't just call it "Yuckmouth."
What does he have?

Answer: Your patient has trench mouth, also known as
Vincent's stomatitis or acute necrotizing ulcerative gingivitis (ANUG). Trench mouth is a painful bacterial
infection and ulceration of the gums.

The term *trench mouth* comes from World War I,
when the disorder was common among soldiers. They
also suffered from trench foot. This was an infection of
the feet caused by cold, wet, and insanitary conditions.
Get out that prescription pad and write an Rx for antibiotics and give the man a toothbrush. Before long his
mouth will glisten again.

DIAGNOSE THIS

Having trouble getting off the couch? Finding it difficult to get anything done?

Answer: Motivational deficiency disorder. Yes, your lazi-
ness may have a medical basis. Australian scientists have

described a new condition called motivational deficiency disorder (MoDeD). It is characterized by overwhelming and debilitating apathy. Scientists at the University of Newcastle in Australia say that in severe cases motivational deficiency disorder can be fatal, because the condition reduces the motivation to breathe.

DIAGNOSE THIS

A large bearded man is sitting in your waiting room and keeps coughing uncontrollably. He has difficulty breathing and you see, under *Occupation* on the medical form, that he is a geologist who specializes in volcanoes. What does he have?

Answer: It could be asthma, but don't forget to consider Pneumonoultramicroscopicsilicovolcanokoniosis. The 2007 edition of *Guinness Book of World Records* listed *pneumonoultramicroscopicsilicovolcanokoniosis* as the longest word in the English language. This refers to a lung disease caused by the inhalation of very fine silica dust from volcanoes. The word has never been used in the medical literature. This word was coined intentionally to be a very long word—oh, those Guiness World Record nerds! In medicine, we would just call it pneumoconiosis.

DIAGNOSE THIS

An 80-year-old man is sitting in your exam room. When you walk in, you notice a large bulge in his right cheek. He has a fruity smell to his breath. You recall that certain smells are associated with disease. Does your nose know?

Answer: Maybe you were thinking that he had an infection in his mouth, diabetes, and diabetic ketoacidosis to account for his fruity breath. Nice try, but this time you are wrong. Turns out he isn't the patient at all. He is just waiting for his wife, Sadie, and having a nice piece of butterscotch candy.

This introduces the following question that actually came up during a slow day in the ER:

Why do grandparents always eat hard candy?

Unfortunately, there is no great explanation for that ubiquitous bowl of candy in Grandpa's house or that handful of Werther's Originals in Grandma's purse. After finishing your coursework at the Why Do Men Have Nipples School of Medicine, you can easily come up with your own new scientific theory. In this case blame it on xerostomia, a dry mouth (it always helps to use big words to drive home the point). Many elderly people suffer from a dry mouth, usually a side effect of the medications that they are taking. A well-placed piece of hard candy helps stimulate salivation and moistens the mouth.

DIAGNOSE THIS

A 51-year-old woman presents to your office with a 2-month history of itchy, slightly red areas on the trunk and extremities. She was previously treated for chronic urticaria (hives), but she hasn't gotten better. She says that she recently noticed a decrease in light touch sensation in the area of the rash and a loss of feeling in her feet. You think you have it figured out, so you order a skin biopsy. When the results come back and show acid-fast bacilli, you give her the news.

Answer: She's got Hansen's disease. It doesn't sound so bad when they call it Hansen's. Leprosy might scare you more, but there is no need to be so terrified. Hansen's disease, or leprosy, discovered in Norway in 1873 by Dr. Gerhard H. A. Hansen, is an infection caused by a bacterium, *Mycobacterium leprae*. This infection is treated with antibiotics. Treatment takes from six months to two years and makes even the most severe cases noninfectious within a few days or weeks. Leprosy is not as contagious as rumored, so the lovely lass won't end up in a leper colony. Approximately 95 percent of the world's population has a natural protection against Hansen's disease. Those who have this resistance will not get Hansen's disease if they are exposed.

Don't confuse Hansen's disease with the painful condition of getting the song "MmmBop" by the Hanson Brothers stuck in your head.

DIAGNOSE THIS

An 18-year-old boy corners you at the local picnic and says, "Dude, I hear you are a doctor, you gotta help me. . . . I keep coughing up these stinky little white things. They look like corn kernels but smell like toe jam. When they fall out, they are firm to the touch and SMELLY." What are those white smelly clumps in the back of his throat?

Answer: Those mysterious malodorous mouth balls are called tonsilloliths or tonsil stones. These hard lumps are formed in the nooks and crannies of the tonsils and contain food particles, calcium and magnesium salts, bacteria, and sometimes small amounts of keratin (the same substance found in fingernails and hair). They contain bacteria that produce volatile sulfur compounds (such as methyl mercaptan and dimethyl sulfide), the culprits in bad breath. They are more common in adolescents, and most people swallow them without ever noticing. Good oral hygiene, gargling, and avoiding eating right before bed may help reduce their formation.

DIAGNOSE THIS

Your next patient is a 44-year-old woman who presents complaining of a dry cough, wheezing, and shortness of breath, especially with exertion. She has no cold symptoms and doesn't smoke, and when you tell her that she might have asthma, she says that is exactly what the last three doctors told her. She adds that she is getting so bad that she doesn't know if she can keep working. You summon your inner medical detective and ask what she does for a living and she replies, "I work in a factory that makes food flavorings." You nod and prepare to deliver your diagnosis.

Answer: You confirm that her plant makes the flavoring for microwave popcorn and then deliver the bad news that she has popcorn workers' lung, or bronchiolitis obliterans. It's an inflammatory obstruction of the lung's tiniest airways, called bronchioles. These airways become severely damaged and inflamed, leading to extensive blockage. The disease can be caused by breathing in a variety of chemicals such as chlorine, ammonia, oxides of nitrogen, or sulfur dioxide. The chemical used to provide the buttery flavor in microwave popcorn, diacetyl, has been linked to this disease. A lung biopsy is the only definite way to diagnose the disease.

Unfortunately, the disease is irreversible, but early diagnosis serves to prevent progression. Severe cases can be fatal if not treated with a lung transplant.

Should you be afraid of your microwave popcorn?
There is one suspected case of a Colorado man who ate microwave popcorn daily for years and had a habit of breathing in those "delicious" but potentially dangerous heated buttery fumes. Apparently, this man had levels of the chemical diacetyl in his home similar to those in microwave popcorn plants.

There is no information that suggests that the average consumer is at risk, but some popcorn makers have opted to remove this chemical. To be safer, avoid breathing the warm fumes or look for a brand that doesn't use diacetyl.

We always thought that the worst thing that could happen from popcorn was that an irritating kernel could get caught in your teeth. Maybe not . . .

CHAPTER 4

Let's start operating! After stretching your brain, learning basic anatomical vocabulary, and honing your diagnostic skills to rival Gregory House, we think you're more than ready to really get your hands dirty.

In the hospital, they say, "See one, do one, teach one." Let's just skip right to the "do one"!

DO-IT-YOURSELF MEDICINE
Appendectomies-R-Us

GREAT MOMENTS IN SELF-SURGERY

Just like great chefs who must sample their own food before they serve it to their customers, great surgeons should always try their techniques on themselves first. Here are a few examples of self-surgery pioneers, all of whom have plenty to teach you.

Slugectomy

In October 2006, Randall William Webb, 42, of Hobe Sound, Florida, and his girlfriend, Janette Brewer, had a dispute with two men from whom they had purchased $20 worth of crack cocaine. In the course of the altercation, Mr. Webb was shot in the right thigh. He proceeded to drive himself home, where he removed the bullet with a box cutter. His surgical assistant, Brewer, assisted in the procedure. She described the intricate surgical technique as follows, "I put some ice on it in a bag to numb it and he cut a little and I cut a little. . . . It was bloody." Afterward they got worried when their surgical colleagues/friends started warning them about lead poisoning and infection. They drove to the emergency room, where doctors checked the wound and gave Webb a tetanus shot, some antibiotics, and a hefty bill.

Mr. Webb is available for ammo removal by appointment only.

Employee of the Month

The following stuff of urban legends was recounted in the July 1991 issue of *Medical Aspects of Human Sexuality*, by Pennsylvania urologist William A. Morton. One morning, a man appears in the ER, his scrotum wrapped in 3 yards of gauze, swollen to twice the size of a grapefruit, bearing a jagged zigzag laceration, and embedded with eight rusty staples. Turns out, several days before, the guy had found himself alone at lunchtime in the machine shop where he worked. He began masturbating by holding his penis against the canvas belt drive of a piece of running machinery. Losing concentration, he leaned in too close and his scrotum was caught between the pulley wheel and the drive belt. Unaware that he had lost his left testis, he stapled the wound closed with a heavy-duty stapling gun. He then returned to work!

If this didn't earn the dude Employee of the Month, then I don't know what will.

Dios Mio!!

A 40-year-old Mexican woman went into labor at home, but was unable to deliver her infant naturally. She then drank three glasses of hard liquor and, employing her well-honed skills at slaughtering animals, used a kitchen knife to slice open her own abdomen and perform a cesarean section, delivering a healthy, breathing, crying male infant. She then asked one of her other children to call a local nurse for help, before losing consciousness. For more details, consult the 2004 edition of the *International Journal of Gynecology and Obstetrics*. (And, *no*, the father was not the guy who stapled his own nut-sack back together.)

Swiss-style Cesarean

In the first recorded incidence of a woman surviving a cesarean section, Jacob Nufer, a Swiss swine gelder, or pig castrator, used his swine-gelding instruments to remove a baby from his wife's womb after a prolonged labor. Not only did Mrs. Nufer survive the surgery but she went on to give birth to twins plus four other children.

Extreme Measures

In April 2003, an adventurous 27-year-old mountain climber, Aron Ralston, entered Utah's Bluejohn Canyon for another rock-climbing expedition. He was climbing alone, when an 800-pound (363-kg) boulder suddenly shifted, crushing his right hand. Pinned against the wall, he unsuccessfully tried several different ways to free himself over the next six days. When his food and water ran out, he realized he'd probably die unless he attempted something desperate. Ralston chose a self-surgery option that made him famous. Using his trusty mulitool knife, he amputated his own right hand, then hiked to freedom. You can read about his "MacGyveresque" operative skills in his book, *Between a Rock and a Hard Place*.

South Pole Survival (Doctor Heal Thyself)

Most of us would probably take a sabbatical from work and head for the beach or the mountains. Not emergency physician Jerri Nielsen. In 1998, the 46-year-old Nielsen sought peace and quiet and a break from her family difficulties by taking a job as the only doctor at a research station in Antarctica. Dr. Nielsen thought she would just end up treating frostbite, but after three months she noticed a lump in her own breast. Dr. Nielsen performed her own breast biopsy, which confirmed that she had breast cancer. It was winter and it was impossible to get airlifted out, so, utilizing airdrops of medicine and equipment, Dr. Nielsen began treating herself with chemotherapy under the guidance of doctors in the United States via videoconferencing.

You can read her whole story in the autobiographical book *Ice Bound: A Doctor's Incredible Battle for Survival at the South Pole.*

Sussex Surgeon Spays Self

Jonathan Heatley, a British GP who specializes in vasectomies, performed his own vasectomy with the help of his wife, a nurse. In 2001, Dr. Heatley proved that British doctors really do have stiff upper lips and steady hands when he completed this 15-minute self-neutering procedure. The General Medical Council denounced Dr. Heatley's self-surgery and urged doctors to avoid treating either themselves or close family members.

MEDICAL SCHOOL FLASHBACK
Surgical Patriotism

There are moments in medicine that are particularly moving, unusually exhilarating, profoundly depressing, and even, on occasion, rousingly patriotic. Yes, patriotic. When I was a third-year medical student, I worked with an amazing surgeon, by the name of Dr. Warren Wetzel, during my trauma surgery rotation. Dr. Wetzel was a unique spirit in the hospital and an excellent teacher. And he had the ability to put everyone at ease, even during the most harrowing times. In his operating room, things always seemed under control. As a medical student, I would watch with awe as he rescued patients from the very brink of death. Needless to say, I had the most marginal of roles in these heroic endeavors. That is, until it was time to "close" (in other words, sew up the patient at the end of an operation). Occasionally Dr. Wetzel would honor his medical students with the privilege of actually doing some of the suturing. Along with this came another task. Most surgeons—Dr. Wetzel included—played music in the operating room. But in his OR, at "closing time," the music was shut off and the medical students had to sing along with what he called "The All-American Closure." Students could choose any patriotic tune, but it had to match his theme of red, white, and blue: red for the red blood, white for the white fascia (a white-colored connective tissue), and blue for the blue-colored suture material (Prolene) that we use to close.

Color-coordinated OR-karaoke may sound silly, but it was surprisingly moving.

—Dr. Billy

HANDYMAN (FIVE-STEP) SPECIALS

DR. BILLY'S DISCLAIMER
Although it's easy and completely harmless for Leyner to go off advising people to diagnose and dissect, I am bound by something called The Hippocratic Oath to DO NO HARM. I know this book is both informative and entertaining, but *please* read this in the spirit it was intended, and don't go and give your roommate a colostomy because you're bored some rainy afternoon. Most instances of self-surgery involve either serious psychopathology or extreme life-or-death circumstance that you are highly unlikely to encounter. To say "Don't try any of this at home" is an understatement.

Do-It-Yourself Hemorrhoidectomy

1. Use retractor to open anus and dilate anal canal.

2. Push gauze swab into anus and then slowly pull it out, causing hemorrhoid to exit with swab.

3. Grasp hemorrhoid in clamp, tighten vein, and cut off mucous membrane.

4. Apply forceps at base of hemorrhoid, squeeze tight, and cut off upper surface.

5. Stitch together edges of mucous membrane (be sure to pull stitches tight) and apply sterile protective dressing.

Do-It-Yourself Liver Transplant

1. Wash donor liver with special solution and cool to 39 degrees Fahrenheit.

2. Make long, vertical incision running from just below breastbone to the navel.

3. Detach diseased liver from underside of diaphragm and gently lift out.

4. Connect blood vessels of new liver to recipient, then connect donor organ with intestinal tract and implant bile duct.

5. Close up incision, sewing each layer—membrane, muscles, skin—separately.

Livin' La Vida Doctor

Writing the Perfect Get Out of Work Note (Advanced)

To Whom It May Concern:

_____ was seen in our emergency room on April 2, 2007. He was brought in by paramedics after being resuscitated in the field from a lightning strike. Paramedics on the scene were able to shock Mr. _____ out of ventricular fibrillation and return his heart to a normal rhythm. _____ was able to inform the attendant paramedics that he'd built a series of ornate Japanese box kites for a group of traumatized central African war orphans and was struck by a lightning bolt as he ran gracefully across a field trying to get one of the careworn children's kites aloft. (This story was later confirmed by the group of tearful orphans who were holding a vigil at _____'s bedside in the hospital.)

In the emergency department Mr. _____ was

observed to have paralysis of the lower extremities. A spinal injury was ruled out and Mr. _____ was admitted to our Intensive Care Unit. The paralysis resolved completely over the course of several days with aggressive rehabilitation. Mr. _____'s only residual injury is a perforated tympanic membrane. He was seen by our ENT service, who recommended that Mr. _____ not travel by air for the next two weeks. Please excuse him from any air travel and also for any missed time at work during this trying time. Also, please understand that lightning victims are prone to emotional liability. It is best that Mr. _____ avoid all stressful situations (such as deadlines, meetings, and . . . work) and be given extremely positive reinforcement throughout the day. Neuropsychiatric manifestations such as memory lapses, peculiar food cravings, and disinhibited sexual behavior MUST be tolerated, and even encouraged.

Yours truly,

Dr. _____

Division of Critical Care Medicine

Beth Israel Hospital

Do-It-Yourself Appendectomy

Note: Many appendectomies are performed today using laparoscopic techniques. These tend to be more resource-intensive procedures than open surgeries—in other words, you'll need a laparoscope, instead of just basically a sharp knife and a needle and thread. If you want, you can purchase a preowned laparoscope online for anywhere between $695 and $1,895, usually with free shipping and handling. But let's just stick to the good ol'-school, tried-and-true, kitchen-counter method:

1. Administer general anesthesia and swab skin of abdomen with antiseptic solution.

2. Through the skin and underlying fat, make a 4-inch-long cut, parallel to and 3 inches above the fold of the groin.

3. Cut open the membranous layer of the peritoneum, and bring the whole cecum (with the appendix attached) through the wound. (Be extra careful to avoid bursting the swollen appendix and releasing its infected contents into the abdominal cavity, which could cause peritonitis and death.)

4. Tie off appendix and cut away.

5. Using a "purse-string" stitch around its base, bury the stump of the appendix within the cecum, and then suture the peritoneum, abdominal muscles, and skin.

Do-It-Yourself Root Canal

1. Administer local anesthesia and secure rubber dam.

2. Drill hole through biting surface at crown of tooth.

3. Ask patient whether he or she has seen any good movies lately, even though patient's responses are completely incomprehensible.

4. Extract contents of pulp cavity.

5. Widen cavity, wash out and pack with antibiotic paste, and seal with temporary filling.

Do-It-Yourself Tonsillectomy

1. Pass breathing tube through nose and down trachea.

2. Grasp first tonsil in toothed forceps and stretch toward front of mouth, then make incision through mucous membrane lining the mouth close to body of tonsil.

3. Strip tonsil from base by separating layer from layer.

4. Suction excess blood and cauterize blood vessels.

5. Repeat procedure on other tonsil.

Do-It-Yourself Tracheostomy

1. Open skin of neck, separate muscles, and cut through central part of thyroid gland. (The thyroid is the thing under the Adam's apple that is shaped like a butterfly.)

2. Cut through cartilage rings that form outer wall of trachea.

3. Insert tracheostomy tube.

4. Replace neck muscles and sew skin edges around the flange of the tube.

5. Apply surgical gauze dressing under flange and secure in place with tape around neck.

HUMOR IS THE BEST MEDICINE

"The practice of medicine is a thinker's art, the practice of surgery a plumber's."

—Martin H. Fisher (1879–1962), German-born physician and author

Do-It-Yourself Vasectomy

1. Inject anesthetic into each side of scrotum.

2. Make a single short vertical incision in scrotum just below root of penis.

3. Inject anesthetic into spermatic cord, and then carefully cut cord to access vas deferens.

4. Pull loop of vas deferens through wound and cut out half-inch piece.

5. Fold back cut ends, tie tight, put back through wound, and stitch incision.

Do-It-Yourself Leg Amputation

1. Cleanse leg with antiseptic solution, and create flaps of skin for later stitching. (Because skin and soft tissue retract, always make incision at least 6 inches below point at which bone is to be cut.)

2. Cut muscle. Clamp and sever femoral blood vessels.

3. Crush sciatic nerve in clamps, tie off, and sever.

4. Saw though femur and round off edge with steel rasp.

5. Close muscles around sawn femur and stitch, then sew together skin flaps.

Do-It-Yourself Carpal Tunnel Syndrome Surgery

1. Make 2-inch-long incision on front of wrist in line with center of ring finger at right angles to crease nearest palm.

2. Hold incision open with retractors.

3. Expose transverse carpal ligament.

4. Using scalpel, cut through transverse carpal ligament to relieve pressure.

5. Close incision with stitches.

Do-It-Yourself Heart-Lung Transplant

1. Attach patient to heart-lung machine. (Skimping on this step will result in the certain death of your patient.)

2. Make incision down center of chest, saw through sternum, and separate halves with retractor, exposing heart.

3. Sever aorta just above heart and cut through trachea ½ inch above point at which it branches to each lung.

4. Remove diseased heart and lungs and replace with donor organs.

5. Stitch trachea and aorta, disconnect heart-lung machine, bring breastbone together, and sew chest wall.

MEDICAL SCHOOL FLASHBACK
Retraction

The operating room is one of the most exciting and terri-fying places for the callow medical student. The OR is extremely hierarchical, with the surgeons at the top of the food chain. Nurses revel in the opportunity to tease inexperienced medical students who are desperately trying to understand the complexities of maintaining a sterile environment. Inevitably, after scrubbing his hands for 15 minutes, and scrupulously donning his surgical gloves and gown, the medical student will find a way to contaminate himself by touching something non-sterile. At that point, a seasoned OR nurse will roughly reprimand you and exile you from the room until you complete the process all over again. Once you've surmounted this hurdle, there are very few other things they'll let you do. Sometimes they'll give you the honor of cutting the ends of the sutures, but invariably you'll get scolded for snipping the ends too short or too long. If you screw up the suture snipping, you'll probably be relegated to retractor duty. (A retractor is a surgical instrument that holds open an incision or holds back underlying organs or tissues.) There is probably not a more boring ordeal than standing in one place for five hours holding back someone's liver with a metal blade. It is not uncommon for the haggard, sleep-deprived med student to actually doze off with the retractor still in his hand. The abuse for this surpasses anything that's happened to the student up to this point.

—Dr. Billy

Do-It-Yourself Rhinoplasty

(Before proceeding, carefully choose the nose you want to use as your design inspiration. Definitely avoid the Bruce Jenner / Ken-doll-from-another-planet look.)

1. Make incision inside nostril.

2. Using a small rasp between bone and skin, file bony hump until contour of bridge conforms to tip.

3. Carve central cartilage into shape with small scalpel.

4. If necessary, gently break side pieces of bridge bone and press inward using small chisel.

5. Suck out blood clots, pack inside of nose with gauze, strap outside, and splint.

DON'T LEAVE ANYTHING BEHIND!

Surgeries where instruments or sponges are left behind are uncommon. The medical literature reports that in approximately 1 in every 1,500 intraabdominal surgeries there is what we call a "retained foreign body."

Gossypiboma (GAWS.i.puh.boh.muh) n. *Gossypiboma* is the technical term for a retained surgical sponge. The word is derived from the Latin *gossypium* ("cotton") and the Swahili *boma* ("place of concealment"). As far as we know, no surgeon has left his watch or car keys inside of a patient.

- -

Do-It-Yourself Breast Enlargement

1. Make incision about 1.5 inches long on underside of breast in front of crease.

2. Reach into tissues, separate layers, and create pocket either in front of pectoral muscle but behind breast tissue *or* behind pectoral muscle, making sure pocket is wide enough to accommodate implant.

3. Position implant in pocket. (Use professional-grade saline implants—the days of bra stuffing with socks or toilet paper are over.)

4. Close incision with several stitches.

5. Repeat procedure on other breast.

Do-It-Yourself Laparoscopic Cholecystectomy (Removal of Gallbladder)

1. Pass needle through navel and inflate abdomen with carbon dioxide gas.

2. Make a 2/5-inch opening in navel for tube—this is the port for your operating laparoscope. (Make

another port incision midline below breastbone and two smaller ports under the ribs.)

3. Free adhesions around gallbladder. Clip and sever gallbladder duct and artery. (The gallbladder is the bile-filled sac under the liver.)

4. Free gallbaldder from underside of liver, transfer laparoscope to upper port, pass forceps through navel port, and pull out gallbladder.

5. Remove ports and stitch openings.

PRACTICING YOUR SURGICAL TECHNIQUE

Step 1. Purchase video game.

Step 2. Play video game.

Step 3. Be a surgeon.

Source (sort of): *Archives of Surgery* vol. 142, no. 2 (February 2007). In this issue of *Archives of Surgery,* you may have read the article "The Impact of Video Games on Training Surgeons in the 21st Century." The authors state that video-game skill correlates with laparoscopic surgical skills and that video games may be a practical teaching tool to help train surgeons. Remember that when your mother tells you to stop wasting your time playing games!

Do-It-Yourself Removal of a Brain Tumor

1. Shave patient's head, cut through skin, and fold back scalp, exposing bone.

2. Use burr drill to make circle of holes in skull. With a Gigli saw, cut bone flap. Hinge flap or lift clear.

3. Tie off blood vessels supplying blood to meningioma.

4. Shell tumor out of its bed using blunt-edged dissector.

5. Stitch dura matter, replace bone flap, and suture scalp incision.

Do-It-Yourself Sex-Change Surgery
(Male to Female)

1. Make V-shaped incision on underside of base of penis and draw back flap of skin, exposing base of penile shaft.

2. Remove testicles and spermatic cords, then strip skin from penis, leaving skin flap attached to body.

3. Using a blunt dissector, make a tunnel for vagina extending from the prostate gland to tissue at base of urethra.

4. Using a scalpel, detach base of penis from pubic bone, leaving small stump for new urethral opening.

5. Create vaginal walls using skin freed from penis, then trim scrotal skin to form labia.

Do-It-Yourself Sex-Change Surgery (Female to Male)

1. Remove breasts, uterus, fallopian tubes, and ovaries.

2. Create penis using abdominal wall tissue.

3. Form scrotum using skin of labia majora.

4. Insert plastic testicles.

5. For erectile function, insert fluid reservoir in abdominal muscles, fluid pump with release valve in scrotum, and inflatable cylinder down length of penis.

Do-It-Yourself Embalming

1. Place body on embalming table, and pack the oral cavity and eyes with cotton.

2. Inject the embalming fluid (generally a mixture of formaldehyde, glutaraldehyde, methanol, and ethanol) into the right common carotid artery, and drain blood from the right jugular vein.

3. Insert trocar (long needle attached to hydro-aspirator) above belly button, aspirate all major organs in torso, and then fill cavity with concentrated formaldehyde solution.

4. Remove trocar, wash body thoroughly, and seal incisions.

5. Dress in stylish yet comfortable attire, coif hair, and apply makeup. (Make sure makeup does not give face a deathly pallor or masklike appearance—keep it simple and natural!)

CHAPTER 5

A ttention, students! You're rounding the corner toward the completion of your time here at the Why Do Men Have Nipples School of Medicine. See how easy it's been to digest and metabolize all this information?! But it's not enough to simply know it all. You have to know how to use the knowledge you've acquired. Before we kick you out of

MEDICAL MANNERS, ETHICS, AND MORALITY
At Least Pretend to Be Professional

the nest to see if you can fly on your own, let's explore some scenarios that illustrate the complexities of maintaining the highest standards of professional conduct.

These days, the eschewal of good manners by physicians seems actually a deliberate attempt to be friendlier and more down to earth, and not so stuffy and officious. But I think young doctors today may be going too far. Comedy has replaced a prudent reserve and gravitas.

How many of you have had to grin and bear some lame prison cavity-search joke when the doctor snaps on that latex glove in preparation for the dreaded prostate exam? Or have you ever been sitting there on that paper-covered exam table in your underwear, when the doctor enters with some *To Catch a Predator* line? ("What do think you're doing here?")

Dentists are notorious for taking comic advantage of your inability to speak. There you are with a Novo-cained mouth full of gauze, mirrors, probes, retractors, and saliva-suction tools, and the dentist elbows you with this salacious smirk on his face. "Your wife's looking superhot lately. Did she get implants?"

What about the simple courtesy of punctuality? What's the longest you've ever waited in the exam room until the doctor finally arrives? An hour? Two hours? Three? By that time, you've done everything possible a human being could do in that room to kill time. You've measured yourself. You've weighed yourself. You've unfurled the sphygmomanometer and taken your own blood pressure. You've even drained your own festering carbuncle—which is the reason you were there in the first place!

Now, not all doctors are inconsiderate and uncouth buffoons. In fact, many are very concerned about improving their manners—bedside and otherwise. Real doctors have traditionally cultivated a noble bearing that evinces a dignified and indefatigably empathic approach to the healing profession. But today we live in an increasingly complicated, globalized, and dizzyingly fast-paced medical world. Challenging and vexing situations arise that can confound even the most unflappable pseudodoctor. When it comes to medical manners and ethics, you need to constantly ask yourself: WWDBALD? *WHAT WOULD DR. BILLY AND LEYNER DO?*

Dear Dr. Billy and Leyner:

I'm an X-ray technologist at a gastroenterologist's office. When I give a patient who's getting an "upper GI" the liquid barium to drink, I like to pour myself a juice or a soda so we can "click glasses" and make a toast. I feel this helps put the patient at ease. Is there anything special I should say?

A: While it's wonderful to be able to extemporize eloquently on such occasions, it's handy to know the standard toasts. Something simple and affable like "Here's to your Upper GI" is always nice. Or you might try something debonair like "*A vos beaux yeux*" (To your pretty eyes). And there are always the old standbys—

"Cheers," "*L'Chaim,*" "*Salud!*" "*Kanpai!*" and "May the road rise to meet you, May the wind be always at your back," etc., etc.

Dear Dr. Billy and Leyner:

I recently performed gastrointestinal surgery on the younger son of a British duke. At the postop instrument count, we discovered that we were one Goligher retractor short. I think I inadvertently left the retractor in his abdomen. I'd like to e-mail the patient and ask him to come in for an X-ray, but I don't know the proper way to address him.

A: First of all, you should know that the younger sons of a duke have the title "Lord" with their first and family names. If you are writing to, for instance, the Lord James Beaumont, address your e-mail "Dear Lord James." Try to adopt a respectful but not obsequious tone, conveying a sense of urgency but not alarm—something like "Would it trouble you terribly if I asked you to stop by the hospital at your earliest convenience?" etc. You could be more specific about the details and say, "It has come to our attention that you are in the possession of one of our finest Goligher retractors. We would be honored to have you return henceforth in order to rectify said matter."

HOSPITAL FLASHBACK
Hard-boiled

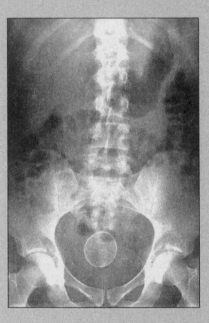

Sometimes it's just not that hard to make the diagnosis. For example, when the note from the triage nurse says "egg in rectum," the patient probably has an egg in their rectum. Yes, this is a true story.

A young gentleman came into the ER complaining of having placed an egg up his butt and then being unable to get it out. Word of the patient and his unfortunate predicament spread through the department like wildfire. Some people maintained their professional demeanor, but others couldn't resist making all sorts of egg jokes—like was it a raw egg that's now hard-boiled or maybe we should just wait for it to hatch, etc. (doctors are not known for their extraordinary comedic talent). After getting an X-ray to make sure that there was nothing else up there (like a chicken), we decided to attempt an extraction. There are some sophisticated techniques that physicians will use to remove foreign rectal bodies, but nothing works better than the ol' tried and true glove-and-lube method. Sometimes we need to sedate the patient, but then it's really just a matter of finding the doctor with the smallest hands in the department.

—Dr. Billy

Dear Dr. Billy and Leyner:

I'm a male nurse in an orthopedic practice in Southern California. A patient—a very distinguished middle-aged gentleman (bowler hat, carved mahogany walking stick)—who'd sprained his ankle playing lawn croquet emerged from the men's room proffering a paper cup of urine. "We don't need a sample," my colleague said to him, brusquely. I thought her remark was rather rude. Am I being too sensitive?

A: Your instincts are impeccable. Your colleague could certainly have responded to the proffered urine in a more gracious way. When offered a cup, accept it courteously and say, "Thank you. How lovely." If the sample is superfluous, dispose of it discreetly, in a manner that is tactful and won't cause the patient any embarrassment.

Dear Dr. Billy and Leyner:

I was given an anesthesia machine (complete with reservoir bags, canisters, connecting pieces, and ventilators) for my birthday earlier this year. I've only used it once and would like to give it to someone as a Christmas gift. Is this considered tacky?

A: No, regifting is now considered a completely acceptable mode of social behavior. But remember, inhalation, exhalation, and the forcible expulsion of secretions create moist conditions favorable to the growth and survival of streptococci, staphylococci, coliforms, fungi, yeasts, etc. So when it comes to anesthesia machines, it's critically important to sterilize the equipment before regifting.

Livin' La Vida Doctor

Sound like an insider by using these playful nicknames that doctors themselves use for other specialists:

Baby catcher or weed puller—obstetrician
Bone heads—orthopedic surgeons

Flea*—internal medicine physician

Gas passers—anesthesiologists

Pecker checker—urologist

Rear admiral—proctologist

Shadow gazer—radiologist

Slasher—surgeon

Stream Team—urologists (also called Wang

Gang and Cock Docs)

Vultures—pathologists (they only show up when

something is dead or about to be)

* There are two reported etiologies of this term:

1. Medical doctors wear their stethoscopes around their

necks like flea collars. 2. Fleas are the last thing to leave

a dying body.

Dear Dr. Billy and Leyner:

I am a cardiac surgeon in Boston. Because of a scheduling snafu, I am performing coronary artery bypass surgery on a patient tomorrow morning and then must immediately attend a formal daytime wedding. I won't have time to change clothes. Would it be considered improper for me to attend the ceremony in my OR attire?

A: Assuming you're a guest and not a member of the wedding party, a wraparound sterile gown worn over the scrub suit is considered proper attire for a formal daytime wedding. Make sure your waistline drawstrings are tucked inside the pants. Any color cap, mask, and sterile gloves may be worn except black, red, or green (which are sometimes considered unlucky). If your face shield is splashed with blood or body fluids, it is considered respectful to doff it as the bride passes your aisle.

Dear Dr. Billy and Leyner:
What if I'm in the middle of performing brain surgery and I have to pee REALLY badly?

A: First rule: Don't drink that extra pint of Guinness while you're at the scrub sink. (In fact, it's probably a good idea to avoid imbibing alcoholic beverages altogether while you're on the job. This is especially true if you're a Norwegian female surgeon. A recent study conducted by the Norwegian Institute for Alcohol and Drug Research determined that female surgeons compared with female nonsurgeons had tendencies for a significantly higher rate of hazardous drinking, and that female surgeons practicing in Norway drink more frequently and more hazardously than other female doctors.)

But back to having to pee REALLY badly . . . Real professionals need to think on their feet. Take astronaut

Alan Shepard, for instance. On May 5, 1961, Shepard was at the controls of the *Freedom 7 Mission,* awaiting to become the first American to travel into space. A series of liftoff delays left Shepard longing to urinate. He radioed Gordon Cooper at Mission Control. "Man, I gotta pee." Shepard wanted to get out and take a comfortable whiz. Given that he was crammed into the confines of a Mercury space capsule atop a Redstone MR-7 rocket at T-minus 15 minutes, a quick trip to the Little Boys' Room was out of the question. Shepard figured he'd just pee in his spacesuit, but Mission Control was concerned that he'd short-circuit the leads. The quick-thinking Shepard had them power off the suit and was free to pee his pants.

With this heroic tale in mind, let's explore your options. You're in the middle of a craniotomy, and you have to pee like a racehorse. What do you do? You could try doing the craniotomy as fast as you possibly can so you can run off to the men's room. That might compromise your surgical technique and jeopardize the survival of your patient. Not good. You could pee in your scrubs (à la Astronaut Shepard), but scrubs aren't as absorbent as a spacesuit. And the pooled urine on the floor could create an electrical hazard while you're using the electrocautery. Our recommendation: Look, dude, you're at the top of the food chain now. Get a medical student to grab a metal surgical bowl and hold it between your legs. This is not the time for false modesty; you obviously need to have your hands free and to preserve a sterile field. Someone—an intern or resident— is going to have to untie your scrub pants, withdraw your penis, and hold it as you empty your bladder. (Norwegian female surgeons may require a second intern or resident to spot them as they squat over the bowl.) Good luck.

LEARN BY EXAMPLE?

There are many physicians who are extraordinary role models. They lead by example, and legions of medical students and residents try to emulate their behavior. Others, well . . . not so much:

Dr. David C. Arndt
In 2002, this orthopedic surgeon joins the hall of shame when he leaves his patient, Charles Algeri, on the operating table to go to the bank to cash his paycheck.

Dr. Abu Hayat
In 1991, Rosa Rodriguez went to this doctor's office for an abortion. She was 32 weeks pregnant at the time and Dr. Hayat began an abortion procedure. He did not complete the abortion on Ms. Rodriguez and told

her to return the next day so he could complete the procedure. That night, she went into labor and her daughter, Ana Rosa, was born with her right arm severed from this hall of shamer's botched procedure.

Dr. James C. Burt

Over the course of more than 20 years, this Ohio gynecologist performed disfiguring operations which he called the "Surgery of Love" on patients, often without their permission. Dr. Burt essentially circumcised his patients with a procedure that involved cutting out the skin around their clitorises and reshaping their vaginas. Finally the Ohio State Medical Board pressured this derelict doc into voluntarily surrendering his license in 1989.

Dear Dr. Billy and Leyner:

I'm a GP in practice in a midwestern inner city. Many of my patients have rather large, elaborate, and often bizarre tattoos emblazoned all over their bodies. For instance, a huge, menacing-looking biker came in complaining of a raging case of jock itch. Examining his crotch for tinea cruris, I noticed that, tattooed on the inner thigh of his left leg, was apparently the movie timetable for showings of *The Notebook* (1:10, 3:40, 6:20, 8:50, and 11:05) at the local multiplex. I couldn't help but ask. . . . He sheepishly explained that he'd been at the tattoo parlor and the tattooist was on the line to Moviephone and didn't have a pencil, so he instinctively reached for the electric tattoo machine, and used his leg as scrap paper. Did I violate protocol by being too intrusive?

A: There's no need to beat yourself up about this. It's okay to ask questions. Patients trust their doctors and enjoy sharing their stories with them. In the medical field, we are privileged to have unique access into people's lives, but there are limits, and you must try to anticipate and respect each individual patient's threshold for privacy. Let us give an example. In 2007, at the Mayo Clinic in Scottsdale, Arizona, a surgical chief resident got himself into hot water for snapping a picture of a patient's privates during gallbladder surgery. The photo, taken during the insertion of a urinary catheter, revealed an interesting piece of body art. The patient, a strip-club owner, had won a bet by decorating his penis with a tattoo that read "Hot Rod." Here's a case where a simple query would have sufficed, but a photograph violated patient confidentiality. You'll learn to gauge your patients' personalities and psychologies. But don't feel as if you have to dampen your natural curiosity—curiosity is a critically important tool for a physician.

HOSPITAL FLASHBACK

Over the years you see some pretty memorable tattoos in the emergency room, but there is one that has burned a perpetual hole in my memory. The patient is one of our frequent visitors and is known to be a rather difficult individual. Nobody ever recalls his real name; he is just known by the two words that are inked onto each of his cheeks: "Pussy Eater."

—Dr. Billy

Dear Dr. Billy and Leyner,

On several occasions, I've farted while I've been examining a patient. It's so mortifying to me, and I'm terribly ashamed of myself. I really feel like it caused some of the patients to lose respect for me as a physician and, actually, one of them never came back. Is there any way that doctors can sort of talk their way out of embarrassing situations like this?

A: First of all, you've got to stop beating yourself up about this. Yes, you're a doctor, but you're also a human being, and now and then—in the presence of a patient—you're going to do human things like fart, belch, cough, sneeze, perhaps even vomit. It's perfectly normal. One of the things you might try is avoiding foods, during office hours, that cause flatulence. Those would be your beans, cabbage, broccoli, prunes, dried apricots, etc. If you're lactose intolerant, steer clear of the dairy products, of course. And remember the rule "Gas in, gas out," and stay away from the carbonated beverages.

And yes, there are simple and effective methods to avoid embarrassment in the event that you do fart while examining a patient. Most important, make it seem intentional, i.e., you need to make it appear as if your farting is a deliberate part of the examination. Ask your patient if the sound was clearly audible or faint. If the patient responds "Faint," then use your otoscope and examine his or her ears. With your tuning fork, perform both the Weber and Rinne hearing tests. Make copious notes on the patient's chart. Then ask your patient if he or she would describe the smell as sweet or acrid. Again, listen carefully to the patient's response, and scrawl notes on the chart. (You might even attach a nasal speculum to your otoscope and give the patient's nose a quick once-over.)

Far from thinking that you've committed some gross faux pas, your patients will assume that you're using the most sophisticated and "cutting-edge" diagnostic techniques available. Chances are, they'll spread the word, and you'll soon have a more crowded waiting room than ever before!

Livin' La Vida Doctor

Writing the Perfect Get Out of Work Note
(Platinum Level)

To Whom It May Concern:

I am a Netsilingmiut shaman from the Adelaide peninsula in Arctic Canada. I met Mr. _____ at a blackjack table at the MGM Grand Hotel in Las Vegas, Nevada. I was there on a junket with a group of other Inuit shamans, including several Utkuhikjalingmiut from Pelly Bay and a couple of Kitdlinermiut from Victoria Island. (The Kitdlinermiut shamans have an evil reputation among our people as murderers and sorcerers, and are traditionally shunned—but, hey, what happens in Vegas, stays in Vegas.) Mr. _____ appeared to be quite careworn and exhausted. He hadn't slept or eaten for quite some time and complained of an intense, unrelieved headache. I agreed to treat him, despite the fact that I hadn't brought any of my sacred paraphernalia and healing amulets with me, like my headdress, sacred belt, and caribou fat. Pursuant to obtaining a brief medical history, I examined Mr. _____ and determined that the pain in his head was due to the fact that his wife's parents had broken two important taboos: his mother-in-law had sewn while an unflensed seal lay on the floor, and his father-in-law had eaten caribou killed with a bow and arrow on the same day that muskox meat was eaten. This had caused evil spirits called *tupiliqs*—which are round in shape and filled with blood—to lodge themselves in Mr. _____'s head. I then followed the standard course of treatment for this condition: I repeated the appropriate magic formulae, went into a trance, and traveled to the underworld, where I enlisted the help of several benevolent ghosts of deceased shamans. The benevolent ghosts then chased the evil *tupiliqs* out of Mr. _____'s head and into a restaurant, where they were serving an all-you-can-eat surf & turf buffet. There, the benevolent ghosts took out their snow knives and cut off the genitals of the *tupiliqs* and ate their livers. Mr. _____ appeared to experience immediate relief. But in order to prevent vengeful *tupiliqs* from returning, I recommend that Mr.

_____ refrain from any type of work (especially work involving harpoons, ice chisels, iron needles, paper, laptop computers, or telephones) for at least a week, avoid any seal meat that has come into contact with menstrual blood, avoid sewing sealskins until the snow melts and the caribou have grown new coats, and, if he has killed a bear with a spear, refrain from cleaning a soapstone lamp for five days to prevent the bear's soul from becoming an evil spirit.

Yours truly,

_____

Dear Dr. Billy and Leyner,

I'm a balding, somewhat portly otolaryngologist in his mid-50s, and I really like to wear my head-mirror and headband out in public. I know there are all sorts of fashion "rules" like "Black and navy blue will never do" and "No white after Labor Day" . . . Are there any rules about wearing a head-mirror and headband?

A: We say: Go for it!! A head-mirror and headband is a classy and timeless look for a fat, bald doctor in his mid-50s! If you want to be très chic, always try to match your head-mirror and headband with your belt and shoes. As far as the etiquette of wearing a head-mirror and head-band in public, there are several important things to keep in mind. Don't push it too far toward the back of your head and make sure it never distorts the natural position of your ears. If you are greeting a woman friend in the street, you should actually lift the head-mirror and headband from your head. But if you accidentally jostle a strange woman in a public place, touch the optical glass of your head-mirror, but don't remove it. Also, if a fat, bald doctor wearing a head-mirror and headband is on any sort of public conveyance (airliner, train, bus, subway, monorail, hovercraft ferry, military Humvee), and he gives up his seat to a woman who is accompanied by another fat, bald doctor who's also wearing a head-mirror and headband, both men should touch the optical glass of their head-mirrors without actually removing them.

Dear Dr. Billy and Leyner,

I'm beginning to question my conduct with one of my patients. He's a man in his early thirties, a derivatives specialist at Goldman Sachs. He's in excellent health, movie-star good looks, six-pack abs, smart, witty, articulate, huge disposable income judging from the Gucci loafers, the Burberry bag, the Porsche Carrera GT, the vacation homes (Aspen, St. Barts) . . . and— oh, did I mention?—in addition to all this, he has an ENORMOUS penis.

I noticed about a year ago when he was in for his annual physical that I was a bit "overly enthusiastic" in my use of the tongue depressor with him, causing him to gag quite a bit. Then when I went to test his patellar reflex (after "searching really hard" for my regular Taylor reflex hammer, I "just happened to find" a meat-tenderizing mallet, and I think bruised his knee a little. On a more recent visit, I "inexplicably" found myself covering his face with gauze and then "inadvertently" spilling a Big Gulp container of Mountain Dew all over it, "accidentally" waterboarding him. . . .

Am I simply guilty of terribly rude behavior, or do you think there's something else—perhaps some envy issues—behind all this?

A: Yes, there could very well be some validity to your suspicion that there's a degree of underlying resentment at the root of your ill-mannered behavior with this particular patient. But you may not be focusing on the core problem here. Lorena Bobbitt notwithstanding, you can't control the size of someone else's penis. You can enhance the size of your own, and you probably should. But the crucial issue here is the disparity between your income and that of your patient. IT'S CONSIDERED INCREDIBLY RUDE AND DISRESPECTFUL TO YOUR PATIENTS TO EARN LESS MONEY THAN THEY DO. Start concentrating on making your practice more lucrative. Obscene prosperity will immediately cure any lingering impulses on your part to torture your patients! Good luck.

Dear Dr. Billy and Leyner,

I'm a doctor in southern Florida. Many of my patients are elderly and suffer, with varying degrees of severity, from some form of degenerative dementia. Occasionally, in the middle of an exam, a patient will forget my name. (A patient recently insisted that I was his son.) Is there a tactful way for me to remind an "absentminded" senior who I am without embarrassing or insulting him?

A: Never say, "You have no fucking idea who I am, do you?"

And in the case of a patient thinking you're someone else—his or her son, for instance—just *be* that person. (Who cares, as long as Medicare and the insurance companies know your real name, right?) For the brief period of time it takes to examine the patient, you'll be able to give him the sublime pleasure of thinking his child is actually a successful doctor instead of some slovenly, unemployed loser who's constantly hitting his elderly parents up for money, which—when he's not passed out drunk in an oblong of sunlight on the carpet of their retirement condo—he immediately loses at the dog track or puts down the G-string of some stripper in Pompano Beach.

Dear Dr. Billy and Leyner,
I still like to give out lollipops to my younger patients. Some of my colleagues rib me for being old-fashioned. Am I woefully antiquated?

A: Giving out lollipops to pediatric patients is a charmingly quaint tradition in our culture, which we salute you for upholding. (We're trusting, of course, that you actually are a licensed physician who's giving lollipops to children you see in your medical office. Pretending to be a doctor and giving candy to children on the street, albeit old-fashioned, is *not* good.)

These are Leyner's favorite lollipops:

- Jolly Rancher Fruit Chew Filled Lollipops

- Charms Blow Pops, green apple flavored

- Sugar Daddies

- ChupaChups

- Tootsie Pops, orange flavored

- Buggin' Glow Pops

- Gummi Fish Lollipop Kabobs

(Avoid giving out fluorescent light sticks along with the lollipops—you will be suspected of promoting "raves." And, by all means, avoid dispensing fentanyl lollipops. Approved by the FDA in 1998 to treat severe pain in cancer patients, they are highly addictive, 80 times more potent than morphine, and have been linked to 127 deaths.)

Dear Dr. Billy and Leyner,

Unfortunately, a thoughtless act of malpractice on my part resulted in the untimely death of one of my patients. What would be considered an acceptable waiting period after which I could begin dating this patient's widow?

A: Is there a better or more infallible guide on matters of such delicacy than the venerable Amy Vanderbilt? "The lonely physician wishing to face realistically the problem of his moral culpability and emotional guilt, today is, after about three months, ready for quiet dates with the bereaved spouse of the patient for whose tragic demise he is responsible. In a small conservative community such dating is limited at first to evenings at home, movies, the theater, musical events, walks and drives, small parties with other couples, but in cities, where life is somewhat more 'modern' and social mores less constrained, drug-fueled, orgiastic saturnalias no longer seem ill-considered or hasty."

Dear Dr. Billy and Leyner,

Is there a polite or decorous way to compel patients to pay what they owe? I have a growing number of patients who are unacceptably delinquent in settling their outstanding bills. My office administrator spends the bulk of her time dunning patients for money. This seems to me like a crass and unseemly way to maintain dignified relationships with men and women under my care. But I don't know how else to handle it.

A: Sending patients threatening letters or constantly calling to upbraid them about unpaid bills is generally considered an uncouth solution to this problem. It manifests a less-than-humane-and-respectful attitude toward your patients, and can only serve to erode these important relationships that you've been so careful to nurture. There is an infinitely more discreet and efficacious way to deal with this situation. Next time one of your defaulting patients is in the office for an exam, make sure he's asked to disrobe and don a patient gown. Keep him distracted, while a nurse rifles through his pile of clothes, quickly removing any cash or credit cards she can find in his pockets. Common diagnostic procedures like chest X-rays or upper GI endoscopies or MRIs— anything that requires a patient to remove jewelry, eyeglasses, or metal objects—are especially conducive to successfully recovering items of value. Do not take more than the amount for which that patient is in arrears. That would be considered exceedingly vulgar.

Dear Dr. Billy and Leyner,
I am a physician in Texas and occasionally, to make extra money, I assist the Texas Department of Criminal Justice in

administering lethal injections to death row offenders. This usually entails cardiac monitoring and examining offenders to confirm death, but on occasion I have also assisted in finding a vein for the IV when the technicians have had trouble doing so. Recently, an incident occurred that continues to bother me a great deal. I was inserting a triple-lumen catheter into the subclavian vein of a death row offender and he complained that I had bad breath. I have always tried to maintain the highest standards of personal hygiene and professional conduct, and this lapse haunts me without respite. What shall I do about my bad breath?

A: Halitosis is a reasonably common symptom that may be the simple result of poor dental hygiene. Certain foods, alcohol, and smoking can result in offensive breath. Dental disorders such as tooth decay, dental plaque, tooth abscess, gingivitis, gum disease, periodontitus, and dentures can also cause bad breath, as can certain throat conditions, including reflux, GERD, and tonsillitis. Different types of breath odor can also accompany more serious medical conditions, such as oral cancer, pharynx cancer, and larynx cancer. A "fruity breath odor" is one of the characteristic symptoms of diabetic ketoacidosis, which can be fatal within hours or days. A "fecal breath odor" can indicate certain types of intestinal blockage.

One other important thing to consider here: The AMA considers physician participation in executions as a violation of core medical ethics. Its 1992 Code of Medical Ethics states that, "A physician, as a member of a profession dedicated to preserving life when there is hope of doing so, should not be a participant in a legally authorized execution." It further states that unacceptable participation includes prescribing or administering medications as part of the execution procedure, monitoring vital signs, rendering technical advice, selecting injection sites, starting or supervising placement of intravenous lines, or simply being present as a physician. Pronouncing death is also considered unacceptable, because the physician is not permitted to revive the prisoner if he or she is found to be alive.

So you might want to seriously consider retiring as a physician and becoming . . . I don't know . . . maybe a serial killer. And if you're still concerned about your bad breath, and think it might be the result of something other than a dental condition or your diet, by all means pay a visit to your family physician.

Dear Dr. Billy and Leyner,
I don't know how to put this without sounding unkind . . . but some of my patients STINK. Their body odor is offensive and almost unbearable. You'd think, in this day and age, most

people would have the common decency to bathe and use deodorant before coming in to see a doctor. But apparently not. I must be going through a case of Febreze a week. Would it be terribly wrong for me to suggest to these people that they take a goddamn shower and slap on some Right Guard if they expect me to examine them?

A: A physician's obligation to his or her patients is to provide high-quality medical care and services, and to be honest, considerate, and polite, and treat them with dignity as individuals. You need to be careful about making subjective aesthetic judgments about their smell. Unless you believe that their hygiene poses a health risk or their body odor is a symptom of some other disorder or disease, you should probably not broach the issue. Unique body odors can be symptoms of certain diseases. Gastrointestinal abnormalities can give the skin a very unusual smell. Diabetics and people with urinary infections will sometimes develop a sweet-smelling or fruity body odor. Scurvy and typhoid fever were associated with strange smells. Specific conditions have their own attendant odors—vaginal and penile discharges, for instance. A smelly ear can be the result of otitis externa, middle ear infection, or cholesteatoma. Even diet can have an effect on body odor—certain foods like garlic, curry, and cumin can cause a distinctive smell.

Some of your patients were simply born with more active apocrine glands than others. Different people have different body odors that are normal for them. And people's grooming habits and their perceptions are informed by a variety of personal and cultural factors. Don't be quite so evangelical about scouring everyone and slathering them with deodorant. Are scrubbed, odorless bodies necessary or even desirable? Pheromones, those airborne chemical signals that waft from our armpits (among other places), convey information about identity, kinship, age, fertility, and arousal. Remember, one person's "stink" is another's aphrodisiac. Napoleon famously wrote Josephine from a campaign, "I will return to Paris tomorrow evening. Don't bathe."

If any of your patients smell like rotting fish, though, you may need to delve more aggressively into the matter. They may be suffering from trimethylaminuria—more colloquially known as fish malodor syndrome. This is a rare metabolic disorder characterized by the presence of abnormal amounts of the dietary-derived tertiary amine, trimethylamine, in the urine, sweat, expired air, and other bodily secretions. Trimethylamine itself has the powerful aroma of rotting fish. Fish malodor syndrome can have an extremely destructive impact on the social lives of affected individuals, and can lead to severe mental depression and, at its extreme, suicidal tendencies.

MEDICAL SCHOOL FLASHBACK
Toxic Sock Syndrome

The emergency room isn't the most fragrant environment to work in. Over time we become immune to the variety of different offensive scents. There is one odor, however, that can bother even the most seasoned ER doctor, the smell of a pair of fermented feet. Over time you come to learn that even when the feet smell bad with the socks on, nothing prepares you for what happens when they come off. This is what we call toxic sock syndrome.

I remember being a naïve medical student and wanting to be compassionate and helpful. It seemed like a great idea to help the nurse clean up a homeless patient. All was going well until I removed those socks. That was when all hell broke loose. The nurse screamed at me and everyone else just scowled at me from afar. I was forced to go up to the operating room to procure a pair of those handy blue shoe covers that they wear in the OR. On that day I learned that you always must have a pair of socks or booties nearby to cover those dogs and lock in the odor or you will face the wrath of all. . . .

—Dr. Billy

MANNERS, ETHICS, AND MORALITY

Dear Dr. Billy and Leyner,

I'm a dermatologist with a thriving practice in Muncie, Indiana. Several weeks ago, I was getting ready to drain an abscess that had developed on the back of one of my patients. As I waited for my nurse to prepare the instruments, I dozed off for a moment or two. My patient noticed, but didn't seem concerned about it in the least. But my nurse has continued to rib me about what happened. She now refers to me as "Dr. Doze," "The Drowsy Dermatologist," "Dr. Zzzzzzz," and "The Somnambulant Surgeon." And she keeps buying mc all sorts of *Snow White and the Seven Dwarfs* paraphernalia with Sleepy circled in pink highlighter. Is falling asleep in front of a patient so terrible?

A: Not only is falling asleep in front of a patient before a procedure not terrible, it's a *wonderful* way of showing that patient how relaxed and confident you are about the ease and successful outcome of the procedure. You should be commended. Alexander the Great pretended to oversleep the morning before his epic victory against the Persians in the Battle of Gaugamela in 331 B.C. It had a spectacular effect on his troops. As the eminent British military historian John Keegan has written, "Sleep in the face of danger, even if feigned, is a magnificent gesture of reassurance to subordinates."

Your nurse's insubordinate behavior, on the other hand, is disgraceful, and she should be flogged.

Dear Dr. Billy and Leyner,

I'm a physician (ob-gyn) in Sparks, Nevada. Over the years I've noticed what a dreary place office waiting rooms can be, so I've made an effort to really "soup" mine up a bit. I've got my nurses in Hooters outfits on roller skates. And I've installed three slot machines (which are a great hit with my patients who are on dopamine agonists and have become compulsive gamblers!). Any other suggestions for making the waiting room a fun place?

A: Sounds like you're on the right track, Doc! (You might want to be careful with that Hooters thing, though. Extremely buxom nurses on roller skates don't have an ideal center of gravity, and can become somewhat unstable. This can result in a lot of spilled urine specimens.) Two other suggestions: thematic music and eclectic magazines. Both are key components of the "fun" waiting room experience.

Here's a list of essential songs the Why Do Men Have Nipples School of Medicine highly recommends for any physician waiting room:

• "Blood Makes Noise" by Suzanne Vega

• "Cancer" by My Chemical Romance

• "Disease" by Matchbox 20

- "Love Like Anthrax" by Gang of Four

- "VD Blues" by Woody Guthrie

- "Whippin' That Old TB" by Jimmie Rodgers

- "The Drugs Don't Work" by the Verve

- "Brain Damage" by Pink Floyd

- "Chemo Limo" by Regina Spektor

- "Cardiac Arrest" by Madness

- "Lithium" by Nirvana

- "21st Century Schizoid Man" by King Crimson

- "Hospital Waste" by Skinny Puppy

- "Why Does It Hurt When I Pee?" by Frank Zappa

- "Like a Surgeon" by Weird Al Yankovic

A varied assortment of waiting magazines is critical. Patients become bored and sullen leafing through the same old, dog-eared issues of *Time, Esquire, Fortune,* and *National Geographic.* Take a look out there at the patients waiting to see you. Beneath their vanilla, heteronormative veneers lie all sorts of eccentric interests and kinky proclivities. Your magazines need to be representative of the latent diversity of your patients.

The Why Do Men Have Nipples School of Medicine recommends:

- **American Cemetery** (an independent trade magazine for cemetery owners and managers offering in-depth coverage of issues affecting the cemetery profession in today's competitive business environment, including grounds maintenance tips, marketing, cremation, and much more)

- **sheep! Magazine** (the Voice of the Independent Flockmaster—covering all aspects of sheep, including raising, caring for, and marketing sheep and sheep products)

- **TWINS** (the premiere periodical for parents of multiples, from twins and triplets to quadruplets, quintuplets, and more!)

- **Prison Living Magazine** (provides articles of inspiration, motivation, and information that prisoners can apply in their unique lives)

- **Unzipped** (the newsmagazine of gay adult entertainment, providing a stimulating mix of nude layouts, party shots, interviews with porn stars, reviews of gay websites and videos, and much more—the quintessential guide for the consumer of gay erotica)

- **Bite me** (if you like vampires, the supernatural, and things that go bump in the night, *Bite me* is the magazine for you)

- **Soldier of Fortune Magazine** (the magazine for mercenaries and professional soldiers, as well as for armchair dreamers and wannabes. "Our editorial policy is pro-military, pro-strong U.S. defense, pro-police, and pro-veteran. We strongly support the right of the individual to keep and bear arms.")

- **Paddles Magazine** (produced by authors and illustrators who speak and understand the language of spanking)

- **D-Cup** (features the world's biggest breasts showcased by bra-busting international models in outrageously explicit pictorials!)

- **UFO Magazine** (a leading source of information in the UFO field, reporting facts about sightings, abductions, and conspiracies)

- **Gamecock** (articles on gamefowl, poultry diseases, sport results, advertising of supplies for proper care of gamefowl, and some history of gamefowl)

- **Whap! Magazine** (Women Who Administer Punishment—the modern woman's guidebook to marital bliss)

- **Meatpaper** ("*Meatpaper* is a print magazine of art and ideas about meat. We like metaphors more than marinating tips. We are your journal of meat culture.")

- **The Pysanka** (articles about Ukrainian Easter eggs)

- **PRO** (*Portable Restroom Operator*—a monthly trade magazine for portable restroom operators)

- **Ferrets Magazine** (providing information about how ferret owners can best care for and interact with their pets)

Livin' La Vida Doctor
"Playing Doctor"

If you're looking to pick up a real medical student, or if you and your spouse/lover/significant other/fill-in-the-blank just want to PLAY DOCTOR at home, here are 10 easy ways to be Dr. Don Juan (or Doña Juana, of course).

1. Ice down your hands prior to any touching.

2. Chill stethoscope to 32 degrees Fahrenheit.

3. Cut off partner's clothes with trauma shears (for more delicate technique, you can use Metzenbaum scissors).

4. Stand in front of naked partner wearing nothing but your head-mirror with headband or binocular loupes (glasses with built-in magnification).

5. Reach down slowly . . . grab wrist . . . and check for radial pulse.

6. Apply nylon cuff of sphygmomanometer, squeeze rubber bulb, and gently inflate cuff.

7. With your freezing cold hands, work your way slowly down the abdomen until you can percuss the lower liver edge.

8. If your partner's been "naughty," sternly tap his/her knee to check for patellar reflex.

9. Whisper in partner's ear that you promise to fully respect patient-doctor confidentiality.

10. Now that the mood has been perfectly set, anything else between the liver and the patella is all you, baby.

Dear Dr. Billy and Leyner,

I have the feeling when I speak to some of my patients about their conditions and treatment options that—even though I try to avoid arcane medical jargon—they are not fully comprehending what I'm telling them. It's very important that they understand their diagnoses, but I don't want to feel as if I'm being condescending and dumbing down what I need to explain to them.

A: In communicating with your patients, absolute clarity is key. We recommend employing whatever linguistic means you have at your disposal for making yourself understood. Modify the scientific complexity of your explanations depending on the medical fluency of the patient. And use the idiom that's appropriate for the age and cultural identity of that particular patient.

For an older, more extensively educated patient, it might be perfectly reasonable to say, "The opening of your appendix into the cecum has become blocked by a fecalith. The major concern here is a periappendiceal abscess or diffuse peritonitis and sepsis. I recommend that an appendectomy should be performed without any unnecessary delay."

The adolescent patient may find the following explanation more accessible: "Your appendix is like, I'm totally gonna rupture. And I'm like, you suck, I'm totally removing you. And your appendix goes, thank you for sharing. And I'm like, whatever."

Or try: "OMFG! WDALYAIC? [Who died and left your appendix in charge?] If we don't take it out now, you'll be ROTFD [rolling on the floor dying]!"

Now, let's say a somewhat professorial gentleman is in your office and you're providing details of his diagnosis and course of treatment. The following might be perfectly appropriate: "Atherosclerotic plaque has built up in the wall of one of the major arteries that supply your heart. The heart muscle in the territory of this artery has become ischemic. And there's concern that a thrombus could form on top of this plaque, completely blocking the artery and causing a heart attack. So we're going to use the saphenous vein from your leg and perform a coronary artery bypass graft in order to create a new route around the blocked artery and allow sufficient blood flow to deliver oxygen and nutrients to the heart muscle."

But if your patient is a wiseguy, a cappo, a mob en-
forcer, then you might very well want to try a different
approach. Because of their constant anxiety about elec-
tronic eavesdropping, men in this line of work tend to
find any sort of conversational specificity very unnerv-
ing. A certain vagueness is called for here. Try something like this: "You know that thing we talked
about . . . that blocked thing? . . . That fuckin' blocked
thing? The thing we talked about? And I told you about
some guy who might be able to do something about
that thing. . . . You know the guy I'm talkin' about,
right? The fuckin' guy who can do something for us
about the blocked thing . . . the fuckin' graft. The guy
who can do the fuckin' graft thing . . . you know what
I'm sayin', right?"

Remember, absolute clarity is *key*.

Dear Dr. Billy and Leyner,
I've found that getting a prostate exam causes many of my
male patients enormous anxiety. Is there anything I can say
before or after the exam that can ease their concerns and dis-
comfort?

A: Of all the procedures that take place in the course of
a routine physical examination, this is the one that strikes

fear into the hearts of so many otherwise stalwart men: the dreaded digital rectal exam (DRE). The snap of that latex glove can turn even Navy SEALs, foreign legionnaires, and ultimate fighting champs into masses of quivering jelly.

The DRE—a procedure in which a physician gently puts a lubricated, gloved finger of one hand into the rectum to check for growths in or enlargement of the prostate gland—should take, at most, about 15 seconds.

But keep in mind that is the only time many men will have someone else's finger—and frequently another man's finger—in their rectums. For many men, this is no big deal, just another minor inconvenience, equivalent to a needle prick or an ice cold stethoscope. But for some, the digital rectal exam is cause for anxiety, teeth-gnashing anguish, and even out-and-out hyperventilating homophobic panic.

Some men writhe in agony as if a swordfish has embedded itself up their rectums. Others turn and give you this look of jaded contempt as if to say, "Is that all you got?"

You're exactly right—the severity of your patient's reaction to the DRE can indeed be assuaged by some well-chosen words, some calming or distracting patter.

Sports (e.g., "So how about those Mets?") is generally considered to be the universal conversational lubricant, easing the way for men to enter into conversation in almost any situation in the world. But it can often seem glib and clichéd. So we recommend against it.

Also, avoid anything that might inadvertently heighten your patient's anxiety. For instance, the conversational gambit "So, you hear about the pervert impersonating a doctor just so he could stick his finger up guys' assholes?" could definitely backfire.

Keep it short and sweet. Don't become enamored with or lulled by the sound of your own voice and leave your finger stuck up some guy's ass as you muse upon some abstract metaphysical concept.

Something mildly provocative is usually diverting. We recommend something along the line of "Was your mother an especially hairy woman?" By the time the patient has a chance to ponder the substance and intent of the question, the exam will be over.

One caveat here: In some cultures this line of inquiry is considered a grave insult. (Oddly, in other cultures it is actually considered an almost requisite social nicety. In a certain nomadic Central Asian tribe, it is considered the depth of bad manners to imbibe even a tumbler of fermented mare's milk without exuberantly voicing the traditional toast: "To your mother's bush!")

The important thing is to be yourself. Avoid canned, prefab, rehearsed remarks. The shelves of drama bookstores are filled with volumes of monologues for doctors performing digital rectal exams. We say, don't waste your money.

When you have your finger in the rectum of a man, in the rectum of an American, speak from the heart. All you need is a snug glove, a silver tongue, and a clean conscience.

MEDICAL SCHOOL FLASHBACK

During the second year of medical school many students get the opportunity to practice examinations on volunteers. When I, Dr. Billy, was in school, that is how we learned to do both pelvic (vaginal) exams and rectal examinations. Experienced volunteers guided us through these procedures for the first time. It was strange and stressful but ultimately a good learning experience.

After "rectal exam day," I went out with some of my nonmedical friends to unwind. We were at a fancy New York gallery opening, sipping wine and telling stories. While I was sharing the details of my day with my friends, I was shocked to see our instructor/the volunteer enter the room. In this case, I avoided any chance of an awkward encounter and slipped out the door . . . luckily unseen.

—Dr. Billy

CHAPTER 6

Nobility of spirit alone is not enough. A somewhat cursory and quasicomplete understanding of physiology, anatomy, diagnostics, and cutting-edge cosmetology are among the essential prerequisites for any fledgling physician-wannabe. This chapter contains your final examination. We are

FINAL EXAM

Test Your Dr. "Skills"

employing the honor system. Please take no more than 45 minutes, use a number 2 pencil, and do not consult any outside references. You are allowed to refer to the textbook, in this case, this book, *Let's Play Doctor*.

At the end of the allotted period, you have two choices: You can either grade your own work (see answer key), or if you wish to receive continuing medical education credit from the Why Do Men Have Nipples School of Medicine, enclose your test results along with a fecal occult blood card from your most recent bowel movement and return them to Carrie Thornton at Three Rivers Press.

Good luck!

1. **Who Am I?**

    I'm a tiny channel or tract that develops in the presence of inflammation and infection. I may or may not be associated with an abscess, but like abscesses, certain illnesses such as Crohn's disease can cause me to develop. I usually run from the rectum to an opening in the skin around the anus. However, sometimes my opening develops elsewhere. For example, in women with Crohn's disease or obstetric injuries, I could open into the vagina or bladder. Sometimes, to find me, a doctor uses an instrument called an anoscope to see inside the anal canal and lower rectum. Who am I?

    Answer: My name is anal fistula. I don't have any friends. Will you iChat or e-mail with me?

2.   Test Your M.D. IQ

What is *Wharton's jelly*?

   A. The gelatinous substance in animals' hooves, horns, and antlers that is used commercially to make candy corn and red licorice

   B. A type of English marmalade cited in the Belle & Sebastian song of the same name

   C. A gelatinous substance within the umbilical cord that is a rich source of stem cells

   D. A slang expression for the business opportunities and networking advantages afforded a graduate of the Wharton School of the University of Pennsylvania

Answer: C

3.   Who Am I?

I'm an abscess in your natal cleft (that would be your butt crack) that tends to become infected and sometimes cause pain and drainage. I'm medically related to a group of diseases known as follicular occlusion. Sometimes I contain hair and sometimes I don't. I can go dormant for years at a time and then flare up. Doctors like to lance me, and sometimes they even marsupialize me.

Answer: I'm a pilonidal cyst!

4. Test Your M.D. IQ

What are the *Islands of Langerhans*?

A. Several small islands in the Caribbean known for their lax banking regulations

B. Bundles of nerve fibers in the inner ear that form the vestibular portion of the eighth cranial nerve

C. A 1983 made-for-television movie starring Hervé Villechaize as a painfully shy, bookish short-order cook who finds himself shipwrecked on a prehistoric island where he is captured by a tribe of buxom, foulmouthed women who don't shave under their arms and use him as their sex slave

D. Cell clusters in the pancreas that secrete insulin and other hormones

Answer: D

5. Who Am I?

Hi. I'm a protrusion of your rectum through your anus. I cause your rectum to turn inside out, so that the rectal lining is visible outside the body. I look like a dark red, moist finger projecting from your asshole. I'm usually caused by straining, such as during a bowel movement.

Answer: I'm a rectal prolapse!

6. Test Your M.D. IQ

What are the *crypts of Lieberkühn?*

A. The place in which Geraldo thought he'd find Al Capone's vault

B. A street gang in Lichtenstein

C. Glands found in the epithelial lining of the small intestine and colon that secrete various enzymes, including sucrase and maltase

D. Fissures in the perineum that can result from excessive use of certain gym apparatus like the Butt Blaster

Answer: C

7. Who Am I?

I'm a fleshy outgrowth of the mucous membrane of your nose. Don't you recognize me? I'm a common teardrop-shaped growth that forms around the openings to your sinus cavities. I resemble a peeled, seedless grape. You may not even be aware that you have me, although you may have nasal congestion, obstruction, drainage, and chronic infections.

Answer: I'm a nasal polyp!

8. Test Your M.D. IQ

An *infarction* is:

A. A violent and egregiously offensive episode of flatulence

B. A moving violation that results in points on your license

C. A congressionally sanctioned naval blockade of an island country that is detaining inebriated American "girls-gone-wild"

D. The death of part or the whole of an organ that occurs when the artery carrying its blood supply is obstructed by a blood clot (thrombus) or an embolus

The answer is D, although common usage has made it acceptable to use "infarction" for all the above.

9. Who Am I?

I'm a mite infestation that produces tiny reddish bumps and severe itching, which is usually worse at night. I'm caused by the mite *Sarcoptes scabiei*. I spread easily from person to person on physical contact. I like to spread through an entire household. It's fun! I love to tunnel in the topmost layer of your skin and deposit my eggs in burrows. My little larvae then hatch in a few days. You'll usually find me in the webs between your fingers and toes, wrists, ankles, buttocks, and, if you're a guy, in your genitals.

Answer: I'm scabies!

10. Test Your M.D. IQ

What's a *precordial thump*?

A. Sexual intercourse before breakfast

B. A firm blow delivered with a closed fist to the lower half of the sternum of a patient in cardiac arrest in order to convert standstill rhythm or ventricular tachycardia to normal rhythm

C. In hockey, a hard, typically blindside check inflicted before the actual game begins

D. The ritualistic shot of peppermint schnapps downed by a Litvak groom and his best man just prior to the wedding ceremony

Answer: B

11. Who Am I?

Wanna hear, like, a story? OK, cool. Your hair follicles, or pores, in your skin contain sebaceous glands that make sebum. Sebum is, like, an oil that lubricates your hair and skin. When your body begins to mature and develop, hormones stimulate the sebaceous glands to make more sebum, and sometimes the glands can become, like, overactive. Whoops! And your pores can become, like, clogged, if there's too much sebum and too many dead skin cells. Then bacteria can get trapped inside your pores and multiply, causing swelling and redness. And that's how I start.

Answer: I'm acne. Duh. Wanna friend me on Facebook?

12. Test Your M.D. IQ

What is the *Annulus of Zinn*?

  A. A lyric from an unreleased Bob Dylan song ("I wait for Nero's fiddling to begin, / As the sun sets over the Annulus of Zinn")

  B. A supermassive region of hypergravity located in the Large Magellanic Cloud (a satellite galaxy of the Milky Way)

  C. The dark, pigmented halo around the anus

  D. A ring of fibrous tissue surrounding the optic nerve, and the origin of the six extraocular muscles

  E. All of the above

Answer: D

13. Who Am I?

I'm an enlargement of your thyroid gland. (Do you even know what your thyroid gland looks like? It's kinda cute—a little, butterfly-shaped gland just below your Adam's apple.) Back in the day, I was most commonly caused by a shortage of iodine in the diet. But since iodized salt was introduced in the United States, this cause has become relatively rare in America. Now I'm more commonly caused by an increase in thyroid-stimulating hormone (TSH) in response to a defect in normal hormone synthesis within your thyroid gland.

Answer: I'm a goiter! (Wanna go up to Inspiration Point and neck?)

14. Test Your M.D. IQ

What is a *Charcot–Leyden crystal*?

    A. An expensive type of Belgian stemware

    B. An accretion of crystallized urine and smcgma that frequently obstructs the urethras of Clydesdale horses

    C. The active chemical ingredient in most commercial toilet-bowl cleaners

    D. A crystal formed from the breakdown of eosinophils (a type of white blood cell), which is seen in the stool or sputum of patients with parasitic diseases

    E. A powdered drink mix developed by NASA in conjunction with French vintners that enables astronauts to enjoy champagne in space (and which is widely extolled in hip-hop lyrics)

Answer: D

15. Who Am I?

When a baby boy is in his mommy's womb, I'm supposed to move down the inguinal canal into his scrotum—but I don't. The fancy-pants name for me is cryptorchidism. Frequently, doctors fix me with a fairly simple surgical procedure called an orchiopexy.

Answer: I'm an undescended testicle!

16. Test Your M.D. IQ

The *MAGPI operation* is:

    A. Meatal advancement and glanuloplasty—surgery to correct hypospadia (a congenital deformity characterized by an abnormally located or incomplete development of the urethral opening)

    B. A 1973 espionage thriller starring James Coburn, Buddy Hackett, and Vanessa del Rio

    C. Make All Girls Pretty Inside—a self-esteem and empowerment program initiated to counter unrealistic standards of beauty for young women

    D. The code name for a covert Israeli military operation conducted in 1991 to rescue Ethiopian Jews

Answer: A

17. Who Am I?

You'll meet me when a portion of your intestine becomes incarcerated or trapped in an abdominal wall defect, and blood flow to your intestines becomes blocked. I'm often very painful and require prompt surgery.

Answer: I'm a strangulated hernia!

18. Test Your M.D. IQ
Medical Reading Comprehension

Read the following and then define each boldface term:

*The patient is a 48-year-old Caucasian male with **DM2, EtOH** abuse with cirrhosis, cervical disc disease, and bipolar d/o who presented with an unclear chief complaint. In the **ED** he was found to have **RUQ** pain and an acute elevation in his **LFTs**. He has had multiple hospitalizations at various local hospitals, and was seen at Mt. Hollywood several days before he presented to Underbrook General. He left **AMA** from MH, which is consistent with all of his discharges from various hospitals. He has left AMA from Underbrook twice and from MH count-*

*less times. He was being worked up at MH for pos-
sible **GI** bleed as **pt** has had a recent drop in **hgb/hct**,
but refused colonoscopy. **EGD** was negative per the
intern there. Pt always requests pain meds throughout
his stay, and has been known to be belligerent and
aggressive towards house staff, requiring several re-
straining orders against him from residents at MH.
Of note, pt used to be a book editor but lost his job secondary to EtOH abuse.*

*Upon admission to the medicine floor, the patient
complained of pain in **b/l** lower extremities, his knees,
and his mouth. He also said his legs were very swollen
and possibly infected. Upon exam, they were indeed
edematous, erythematous, warm to the touch, and
tender, so he was also placed on **Ancef** for **cellulitis**. Pt
became increasingly belligerent and bizarre and Psychiatry saw patient on HD#4 and they said pt was
not a danger to self or others, and further evaluation
should be made when pt was medically stable. Pt was
not put on any psych meds, and he says he has not
taken them for over 10 years. Psych requested an
NCHCT which did not indicate a subdural he-
matoma (pt said he fell a few days ago).*

*The patient eloped on HD#6. He was last ob-
served with a **BLT**. If pt returns to hospital, would
recommend continuing antibiotics for cellulitis.*

Answer Key

DM2—diabetes mellitus type 2

EtOH—chemical abbreviation for alcohol

ED—emergency department

RUQ—right upper quadrant

LFT—liver function test

AMA—against medical advice

GI—gastrointestinal

pt—patient

hgb/hct—hemoglobin and hematocrit (measures for anemia)

EGD—esophagogastroduodenoscopy

b/l—bilateral

edematous—swollen

erythematous—red

Ancef—cefazolin (an antibiotic)

cellulitis—skin infection

NCHCT—noncontrast head CT (CAT scan, computed tomography)

BLT—bacon, lettuce, and tomato sandwich

19. Who Am I?

I'm a noncancerous skin growth that occurs on the soles of your feet. I'm caused by the human papillomavirus (HPV). Sometimes I look like a little cauliflower with black pinpoints (these are actually tiny, clotted blood vessels).

Answer: I'm a plantar wart!

20. Test Your M.D. IQ

True or false? Martin Van Buren, the eighth president of the United States, had no bones or cartilage in his face. As a result of this abnormality, his face had the consistency of soft clay. This meant that it would become misshapen if kissed too roughly or handled at all. Sheet marks would last until his face was smoothed. If he slept on one side all night, he would wake up with that side of his face completely flattened. A sculptor was retained by the White House to remold Van Buren's face every day.

Answer: False

21. Who Am I?

I'm a greenish yellow fluid secreted by your liver and stored in your gallbladder. I have a lot of "issues." I'm bitter because you never, ever think about me. You always think about your blood and your cerebrospinal fluid . . . but never me! Even though I play a crucial role in the intestinal absorption of fats! Try doing without me after you eat a Huevos Rancheros Breakfast Burrito!

Answer: I'm bile! (Like you care.)

22. Test Your M.D. IQ

What is the *sphincter of Oddi*?

A. The viselike crevice within the anus of the mythological Norse monster Oddi, in which the thunder god Thor was imprisoned for 40 days and 40 nights

B. A sphincter muscle situated in the duodenum that controls the influx of bile and pancreatic secretions into the bowel

C. A 69.42-carat pear-shaped diamond given to Elizabeth Taylor by Richard Burton as an engagement gift

D. A seemingly meaningless phrase scrawled on a men's room stall in a rest stop on the New Jersey Turnpike

Answer: B and D

23. Who Am I?

I'm a fluid-filled sac surrounding a testicle that results in the swelling of your scrotum. Do you want a hint? The third syllable of my name sounds just like the name of Heidi Klum's husband.

Answer: I'm a hydrocele!

24. Test Your M.D. IQ

What do Al Roker, Roseanne Barr, Carnie Wilson, Randy Jackson, and Sharon Osbourne have in common, aside from the fact that they've all had bariatric surgery?

Answer: Absolutely nothing.

25. Who Am I?

I'm the foul-smelling, cheesy accumulation of desquamated epidermal cells and sebum that accumulates in the moist areas of the genitalia, especially in uncircumcised males.

Answer: I'm smegma, dude!

26. Test Your M.D. IQ

True or false? Stephen Foster, the American song-writer and composer responsible for such enduring favorites as "Oh! Susannah" and "Camptown Races," had jet black hair growing from one armpit and bright red hair growing from the other—a genetic anomaly that occurs in only one out of five million people.

Answer: False

27. Test Your M.D. IQ

True or false? Neville Chamberlain, the British statesman whose controversial policy of appeasing Adolf Hitler resulted in the 1938 Munich Pact, refused to keep his contact lenses in the customary plastic storage case, preferring, instead, two rain-filled hoofprints.

Answer: False

28. Test Your M.D. IQ

Human beings detect taste with taste receptor cells that are clustered on taste buds located on the surface of the tongue. There are five primary taste sensations. Select the five from among the following:

A. Salty

B. Tart

C. Sour

D. Rancid

E. Peppery

F. Cap'n Crunch

G. Sweet

H. Bitter

I.   Like chicken

J.   Slim Jim

K. Umami (response to salts of glutamic acid, like MSG)

Answers: A, C, G, H, and K

29. Test Your M.D. IQ

Chyme is:

    A. The Chaucerian (i.e., Middle English) spelling of the word *charm* as in *chyme bracelet* and *Lucky Chymes—They're Magically Delicious!*

B. The first secretion from the breast (before the formation of true milk) containing serum, white blood cells, and protective antibodies

C. A Jewish drinking toast, meaning "To life!"— immortalized in the 1983 film *Yentl* starring Barbra Streisand and Mandy Patinkin, in which Yentl (aka Anshel) is seated at a bar in Tombstone, Arizona, lifts a Pink Elephant (a borscht shot with Jäggermeister) and says, "L'Chyme, bitches"

D. The semiliquid acid mass that is the form in which food passes from the stomach to the small intestine

Answer: D

30. Test Your M.D. IQ

The *canal of Nuck* is:

A. The 19-minute magnum opus on the Yes album *Close to the Edge*

B. A canal traversing the Isthmus of Nevis, upon which Vice-Admiral Horatio Nelson—commanding the 64-gun frigate *The Chronic*—uttered the immortal words "This gland that is

England," whereupon he was decapitated by a cannonball

C. An abnormal patent pouch of peritoneum extending into the labium majus of women

D. A river of molten onyx on the banks of which Isildur cut the One Ring from Sauron's hand with the hilt-shard of Elendil's broken sword Narsil in J.R.R. Tolkien's *The Lord of the Rings*

Answer: C

31. Test Your M.D. IQ

McBurney's point is:

A. The precise location on the perineum that is equidistant from the anus and the urethral opening

B. The scenic spot in *Happy Days* where Joanie and Chachi used to make out

C. The point on the abdomen that overlies the anatomical position of the appendix and is the site of maximum tenderness in acute appendicitis

D. The famous syllogism devised by Seamus McBurney, a professor of logic at Trinity College in Dublin ("All men are mortal. Richard Simmons is a man. Therefore, Richard Simmons is mortal.")

Answer: C

32. Test Your M.D. IQ
True or false:

• Although eyeglasses enable you to see better, they cause vision to worsen over time.

• Overuse of the eyes damages vision.

• Eye exercises can improve vision.

• Over-the-counter reading glasses hurt the eyes.

• Wearing contact lenses will prevent nearsightedness from getting worse.

• Eating carrots can improve vision.

• Using night-lights in infants' rooms will make them nearsighted.

Answer: All these statement are false.

33. Test Your M.D. IQ

Strongyloides are:

- **A.** A form of glycogen stored in slow-twitch muscles for use in lifting extremely heavy weights

- **B.** A parasitic roundworm that lives in the mucosa of the small intestine

- **C.** The identical-twin Samoan tag team that defeated Hardcore Holly and Cody Rhodes in a steel-cage death match for the WWE Championship

- **D.** A powerful new kind of Altoids made from the *Mentha requienii*, a species of mint native to Corsica and Sardinia

Answer: B

34. Test Your M.D. IQ

Match the common ailment with its medical name:

Dandruff	Epistaxis
Jock itch	Pruritus ani
Prickly heat	Tinea cruris
Anal itch	Pityriasis capitis
Nosebleed	Miliaria rubra

Answer: dandruff = pityriasis capitis; jock itch = tinea cruris; prickly heat = miliaria rubra; anal itch = pruritus ani; nosebleed = epistaxis

35. Test Your M.D. IQ

What is *puerperal fever*?

    A. An elevation in temperature from consuming a kind of shellfish yielding purple dye

    B. A moving number from the English hard rock band Deep Purple

    C. Childbed fever, which lasts for more than 24 hours within the first 10 days after a woman has had a baby

    D. A tree illness that ravaged the North American elm caused by the pupal stage of the gum moth

Answer: C

36. Test Your M.D. IQ

Who first accurately drew the uterine artery and the vasculature of the cervix and vagina?

    A. Galen

    B. Leonardo da Vinci

    C. Gabriello Falloppio

D. Pier Paulo Pudenda

E. William Hanna and Joseph Barbera

Answer: B

37. Test Your M.D. IQ

Cocosmia is:

    A. A cocktail made by combining cognac, absinthe, crème de cacao, and banana purée

    B. The hallucination of foul odors

    C. A Ukrainian reality show in which a nubile young woman (who wrote her doctoral thesis on Alexander Pushkin's verse novel *Eugene Onegin*) is sent to work on an oil rig in the Caspian Sea with 10 desperately horny and basically illiterate men

    D. The great-granddaughter of Coco Chanel (and Nicole Ritchie's BFF)

Answer: B

38. Test Your M.D. IQ

Papulosquamous is:

    A. The Lenni Lenape term for "a woman who overindulges in deer-jerky"

B. The paterfamilias of the Smurf family

C. A rash that is both papular and scaly, e.g., pso-
riasis

D. Writer of *My Big Fat Greek Wedding*

Answer: C

Scoring Key

34–38 correct: tenured position at the Johns Hopkins
School of Medicine

30–35 correct: senior member of the writing staff on
Animal Planet's *Emergency Vets*

20–29 correct: executive director at the Steve
McQueen Institute for Laetrile and High Colonic
Research in Tijuana, Mexico

10–20 correct: freshman at the Suzanne Somers
Academy of Homeopathic Thigh Mastery in Malibu,
California

0–10 correct: Congratulations! You are the new intern
for Dr. Billy Goldberg and Mark Leyner. Please wear a
hair net and sensible shoes.

Ladies and Gentlemen, today is a momentous and joyous occasion here at Bedside Manor and throughout the hallowed halls of the Why Do Men Have Nipples School of Medicine. As we look out at the audience this afternoon, in addition to seeing the proud faces of our graduates, we can't help but notice the glowing pride and relief on the faces of friends, family members, and creditors.

COMMENCEMENT ADDRESS

Today, You Are a Real Fake Doctor

It has not been an easy road . . . wait a minute . . . it's been ridiculously easy. That's been the whole point! But that doesn't diminish the extent of your accomplishments. Today marks the end of one chapter (six actually, seven if you count this one) and the beginning of another in the lives of each and every one of you. Today marks your first day as a Real Fake Doctor.

Let's think back to your time here at Bedside Manor. We've tackled some remarkably difficult subjects. Before you enrolled, your brain was a tabula rasa—a blank slate—but now you have the supercharged, crackling cerebrum of a Real Fake Doctor. Before you enrolled you didn't know your thymus from your thyroid. Now you could pick out the guilty guy with the multinodular goiter in a police lineup. Before you enrolled, you couldn't change a lightbulb. Now you can perform a successful pancreaticoduodenectomy in the cozy confines of your own garage.

In order to have achieved these accomplishments, you've had to make an enormous investment. But everything comes at a price. If we were to ask the members of this audience what debt they've accumulated in pursuit of their dreams, we would hear from the college grad who owes the National Guard four years of required service, we'd hear from the compulsive gambler who's into his loan shark for 150 Gs, or we'd hear the plaintive wail of the anesthesiologist who's facing the prospect of paying off his $200,000 medical school debt.

But you, our students . . . yes, you have invested your time, you have invested your energy . . . but what will you owe? $200,000? $50,000? $5,000? *No!* Merely the measly $14.95 (if you were actually stupid enough to have paid full price) you shelled out for this invaluable volume.

So why waste any more of your time? The moment has come for all of you fledgling fakers to leave the confines of the nest and spread your wings.

We'd like each of you to repeat these words silently to yourself: "Today I am a Real Fake Doctor." Feels good, doesn't it? Remember, just say this silently to yourself. Other people don't really need to know all the details.

Now it is time to take the oath of the Real Fake Physician (adapted from the Declaration of Geneva of the World Medical Association and reduced to five easy-to-remember steps):

1. I solemnly pledge myself to use my limited knowledge in the service of humanity (and to impress my family, friends, and coworkers);

2. I will give my teachers the respect and gratitude that is their due (and 10 percent of all future earnings payable in money order or cashier's check to Mark Leyner and Dr. Billy Goldberg);

3. I will practice my profession ~~with conscience and dignity;~~

4. I will maintain, by all the means in my power, the honor and the noble traditions of the (real fake) medical profession;

5. I make these promises solemnly, freely, and upon my honor.

You may now leave the premises. (We have another class graduating in 15 minutes.)

The Why Do Men Have Nipples School of Medicine

DIPLOMA

The Trustees and Faculty of the University,
by virtue of the authority vested in them, have conferred on

(Your Name Here)

who has satisfactorily pursued the Studies and passed the
Examinations required therefore the Degree of

Real Fake Doctor of Medicine

with all the Rights, Privileges, Honors,
and Responsibilities thereto appertaining.

Billy Goldberg
Dr. Billy Goldberg
Dean, Clinical Affairs

Dolores Guittlerez
Dolores Guitterez
Housekeeping

Mark Leyner
Mark Leyner
Dean, Student Life

ACKNOWLEDGMENTS

Billy:

I wish to thank my loving family for all their support. To my wife, Jessica: You married an Olympic gold medalist in complaining. Thank you for supporting my pursuit of this difficult sport. I love you. Brody, you are funnier and more inspiring than I ever imagined a two-year-old could be. Thanks for laughing at my "funny jokes." To Lucy, the newest addition to the Goldberg clan, your sweet smile brightens up every day.

(I was just reading the acknowledgments of our first two books and realized that I never properly thanked Leyner, the smartest and quirkiest friend imaginable—a fake doctor extraordinaire. Mark, what a glorious run we are having. You are a genius, an inspiration, and an outstanding friend. I'm so glad that we get to share this amazing ride together.)

Mark:

Thanks to my wife, Mercedes, my daughter, Gaby, and my great, wonderful, eternal Nipple Brother, Billy Goldberg.

Together we would like to thank . . .
Carrie Thornton, Amanda Urban, Jay Sones, Shawn
Nicholls, Philip Patrick, Donna Passannante, Annsley
Rosner, Robert Siek, Dan Rembert, Maria Elias,
Nupoor Nagle, Nickie Sprinkle, Jill Flaxman, Jenny
Frost, Liz Farrell, Heather Bushong, Clay Ezell, and
Alison Schwartz.

ABOUT THE AUTHORS

MARK LEYNER is the author of five books: *Et Tu, Babe; My Cousin, My Gastroenterologist; Tooth Imprints on a Corn Dog; I Smell Esther Williams;* and *The Tetherballs of Bougainville.* He has written scripts for a variety of films and television shows, and recently cowrote the movie *War, Inc.*

BILLY GOLDBERG, M.D., is an emergency medicine physician at Bellevue Hospital and NYU Langone Medical Center in New York. He is an assistant professor in the Department of Emergency Medicine at the NYU School of Medicine. He is also the host of his own weekly show on Sirius Satellite Radio's Doctor Radio channel. In addition to his writing, Billy is an accomplished painter whose works are held in collections in New York, San Francisco, Sydney, and Madrid.

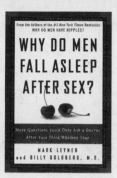

The doctor is in! Again! This time taking on the differences between the sexes

Get the real lowdown on everything everyone wants to know, like:

- Does peeing in the shower cure athlete's foot?

- Can you breast-feed with fake boobs?

- Does thumb sucking cause buckteeth?

- Do your eyebrows grow back if shaved?

WHY DO MEN FALL ASLEEP AFTER SEX? • 978-0-307-34597-4 •
$13.95 paper (Canada: $18.95)

THREE RIVERS PRESS • NEW YORK

Available from Three Rivers Press wherever books are sold.
www.crownpublishing.com

Dedication Answer Key

1.	L	19.	P
2.	R	20.	E
3.	X	21.	GG
4.	AA	22.	M
5.	FF	23.	S
6.	BB	24.	EE
7.	C	25.	Q
8.	T	26.	J
9.	U	27.	H
10.	DD	28.	II
11.	HH	29.	F
12.	B	30.	JJ
13.	CC	31.	A
14.	W	32.	N
15.	I	33.	O
16.	D	34.	V
17.	Z	35.	G
18.	K	36.	Y